desserts
from my
kitchen

LESLEY STOWE

desserts
from my
kitchen

from the creator of
raincoast crisps®

BARLOW

Library and Archives Canada
Cataloguing in Publication data
available upon request.

ISBN 978-0-9937656-0-5 (print)

Printed in Canada

ORDERS:
In Canada:
Jaguar Book Group
100 Armstrong Avenue
Georgetown, ON L7G 5S4

In the U.S.A.:
Midpoint Book Sales &
Distribution
27 West 20th Street, Suite 1102,
New York, NY 10011

SALES REPRESENTATION:
Canadian Manda Group
165 Dufferin Street, Toronto, ON
M6K 3H6

Cover and interior design:
   Mauve Pagé/Page & Design
Photography: Danielle Acken/
   D.L. Acken Photography
Food styling: Tami Hardeman
Production and editorial:
   Tracy Bordian/At Large
   Editorial Services

Visit the author's website
at www.lesleystowe.com

For more information, visit
www.barlowbookpublishing.com

Barlow Book Publishing Inc.
96 Elm Avenue, Toronto, ON,
M4W 1P2

BARLOW

For my parents,
with love.

about the author

Lesley Stowe is a well-known Vancouver chef and the creator of the famous Raincoast Crisps—one of Oprah's "10 Favorite Things." Before becoming the Queen of Crisps, Stowe ran a highly successful catering and food store in Vancouver that became famous for such delectable desserts as Death by Chocolate, served at Vancouver's top restaurants.

A Paris-trained chef, Stowe has published several successful cookbooks, including *The Lesley Stowe Fine Foods Cookbook*. Stowe shares her tips for delicious cooking and entertaining on shows like *Entertainment Tonight Canada* and *CTV Morning Live*.

also by lesley stowe

The Lesley Stowe Fine Foods Cookbook

contents

preface

When I came home to Vancouver from cooking school in Paris, I noticed that something was missing. It was desserts, the kind of elegant, sophisticated desserts that I had learned to make at l' Ecole de Cuisine La Varenne. I longed for the tarte tatin and the contrast it set up between the sweet buttery texture of pastry and the complex caramel of apples that have been simmered forever. I could still taste those flourless chocolate cakes we made with the darkest bittersweet chocolate. They could satisfy my craving for chocolate in just a couple of bites. Yet back in the 1980s, in the spectacular city of Vancouver where I grew up, I couldn't find these delectable desserts in most restaurants. Most of the top restaurants couldn't afford their own pastry chefs or didn't have the kitchen space, so they would order out, and what they bought was typically big, clunky desserts—carrot cake, cheesecake, and basic chocolate cake. Popular, perhaps, but not very inspiring. This was a need I was in a great position to fill.

Settled back in Vancouver, I'd set up my own catering business, but as a young and entrepreneurial chef, I needed to find a way to stand out and stay busy during the slow months. When I realized that the city's restaurants were not offering innovative and refined desserts with high-quality ingredients, my mission was clear.

The challenge was to make a simple and elegant dessert for North American tastes, something with a wow factor. Back in my kitchen, I began to work on some of the French recipes I loved so much, and one of my first creations was Death by Chocolate. It was a chocolate terrine, cranked up for the North American market. This was something new for food lovers in Vancouver (flourless chocolate cakes had not yet become a staple of the dessert menu). The name came from the people who tried it: "Wow," they'd say, "this is to die for." Death by Chocolate was a hit, and Bishops, the restaurant that served it up, added a dramatic flourish by splashing raspberry coulis on the plate. People loved it. I'm told that Pierre Elliott Trudeau always ordered two servings.

Another new recipe came about when a friend of our family was getting married and planning a Hawaiian honeymoon. In the spirit of that adventure, we made a papaya passion fruit tart. It was fresh, citrusy, and rich all at the same time.

I imagined it as an exotic journey though tastes and textures, with one surprise after another as you tasted the fresh papaya, the rich orange almond filling, the passion fruit cream, and the sweet apricot glaze, all in one spectacular dessert. It became another signature dessert, both for us and for the restaurant that served it.

By 1990, I wanted customers to be able to buy direct from me, rather than ordering desserts at the end of a meal in a restaurant, so I opened a shop on 3rd Avenue in Vancouver, near Granville Island, the city's prime food market. It was more than just desserts, though—it was a full-fledged specialty food store, with great cheeses from Italy, France, Spain, and the United States, as well as unpasteurized cheeses, which were new to Vancouver. We were culinary pioneers in a city where specialty food stores usually meant delis with a couple of kinds of salami and basic cheeses. People would come to pick up dinner—fresh crab cakes with caper aioli, perhaps, with grilled vegetables, our own artisanal bread, a bottle of olive oil from Badia a Coltibuono, and, to finish it off, a tangy lemon soufflé tart.

By then we were re-inventing the wedding cake, which traditionally was a fruitcake or sometimes a chocolate or vanilla cake. In those days, people often didn't eat the cake; they'd take home a little bit in a napkin. I thought the wedding cake should be the hit of the evening, from a culinary point of view of course. Back in my kitchen, I came up with all kinds of cakes—everything from a dense, flourless chocolate sponge layered with hazelnut meringue, ganache, and raspberries, to a lemon biscotti mousse cake layered with cream and blackberries, to a Champagne sabayon cake covered in a cascade of white chocolate curls.

We revelled in the finishes that made these cakes so spectacular. One of our pastry chefs was an artist, so the cakes turned into works of hand-crafted art, with quilted squares made of rolled fondant, candied silver beading, real gold and silver leaf, and fondant ribbons. For one wedding we literally went over the top. This was the Mad Hatter cake, a topsy-turvy concoction, with layers of wild color and design—polka dots, checkerboard, and daisies, just for starters. It looked like it was about to topple over, but it never did.

Making these cakes was sometimes a challenge. Vancouver can get hot in the summer, and since we had no air conditioning in our kitchen, we'd have to put on winter coats and work in our giant cooler to make sure our designs didn't melt before we sent them out.

I took cakes all over the place. One time I flew with the cake, in layers, to my cousin's wedding in California. This was before the rigorous checking at the border, and the customs officials thought it was funny to see someone flying south with boxes of cake. We made it, the cake and I, but then I nearly squished the pieces while my husband was driving too quickly on the curvy roads to Napa. It all turned out well, though. The cake, a chocolate cake with layers of hazelnut praline, ganache, and buttercream covered in fondant and flowers, was the hit of the evening. The bride saved the top layer in her freezer for their first-year anniversary.

Other trips were more treacherous. I had to deliver a cake to my father's boss's house in West Vancouver, which was across the waters of English Bay from our kitchen. The cake was for the boss's daughter, who was getting married. The cake

survived the trip to the destination, but when I got out of the car with the cake in my arms and climbed up the stairs through a rockery garden, I missed the hose that had been left lying at the top of the stairs. I tripped, and three layers of buttercream cake almost landed on the ground. I raced back to my kitchen, a 45-minute drive away, reconstructed the cake, and got it back in time for the toasts.

Another time, I delivered a gorgeous white chocolate almond wedding cake to the University of British Columbia. It's one of the most beautiful sites in Canada, and it was a spectacular day. You could see the snow-capped mountains across the water. The cake looked splendid. When we got back to the kitchen, I got a frantic call from the wedding planner. They had changed the venue, without telling us!

After a few years of delivering desserts all over the city, I saw a completely different opportunity. We used to make a graham bread that we would slice thinly and serve with smoked salmon, and I thought we should dry the slices out and improve upon the standard dried bagel thins and melba toast. We eventually tweaked the recipe by adding seeds, rosemary, and other seasonings. People lined up around the block to buy the crisps at our store, and eventually I decided to focus on this popular new product. So began the wonderful story of Raincoast Crisps, which eventually were sold in 4,000 stores in North America and won a coveted spot on Oprah's ten best things of 2012. One year later, our Salty Date and Almond Raincoast Crisps were named the outstanding cracker of the year at New York's Fancy Food Show. We won the Sofi, the specialty food world's version of an Oscar.

Desserts, though, were always in the back of my mind. I have a big sweet tooth, and, as a keen cyclist and skier, I feel that if you're going to indulge in calories, the dessert might as well be the best. I love making desserts for my family and friends in my own kitchen. In summer, I go for the luscious berries and fruits when they're at their peak. I like to pair blackberries and raspberries with an amazing almond cake and crème fraîche. So delicious. In winter, I turn to sticky toffee pudding, autumnal fruit clafouti, chocolate bread pudding with dried cherries and port, or a gingerbread cake with caramelized pears. So great on a cold day after a hike or a ski.

Lots of friends have been asking me for the recipes for my desserts, especially after I stopped making them for weddings, for restaurants, and for my own store. I included Death by Chocolate in my 2006 cookbook, *The Lesley Stowe Fine Foods Cookbook*, but I still yearned to do a cookbook just about desserts. It's been satisfying to fulfill that dream. Throughout this book you'll find not only all of my favorite creations, but also For Best Results pointers—tried-and-tested tips from my professional kitchen—to help you in your kitchen. (You can also look for instructional videos on my YouTube channel.)

Many people are intimidated by the prospect of making desserts, so they go to a store to buy them, even if they're cooking the rest of the dinner. You don't have to! I'm hoping to bring desserts back into the family kitchen. It's fun to cook with friends and family, and can be very comforting, even therapeutic. It's an easy way to connect and be together. Once you're done, when you bring out the dessert, you'll enjoy the accolades. People will remember that dessert for a long time. I hope this book inspires you to get in your kitchen and have fun!

—Lesley Stowe

in my pantry

Having a well-stocked kitchen will give you the flexibility to make all types of desserts without an excessive amount of preplanning or trips to multiple stores. Here's what I like to keep on hand.

dry pantry

Flour

ALL-PURPOSE FLOUR: Most of my recipes call for unbleached all-purpose flour. All-purpose flour is a blend of hard and soft wheat and has a gluten content of 10% to 12%.

CAKE FLOUR: Cake flour is made from soft wheat and has a gluten content of about 8%. It's most often used to make delicate cakes and cookies.

Leavening Agents

Leavening agents are used in doughs and batters to help them rise. They are what give baked goods their soft, sponge-like textures.

BAKING SODA/SODIUM BICARBONATE: Baking soda is activated by the introduction of an acid and a liquid, which causes it to release carbon dioxide into the dough or batter as it is baking and form air bubbles. Baking soda has a shelf life of about 1 year. To test if yours is still active, mix a spoonful of baking soda in lemon juice or vinegar—it should bubble up furiously.

BAKING POWDER: Baking powder is a combination of baking soda, two acid salts—monocalcium phosphate and sodium aluminum sulfate (one reacts to liquid and the other reacts to heat)—and cornstarch. It functions similarly to baking soda, but only requires the addition of a liquid to trigger a reaction. You can find some varieties of aluminum sulfate–free baking powder at health food stores, but you can also make your own baking powder at home. Simply combine 1 tsp (5 mL) cornstarch, 1 tsp (5 mL) cream of tartar, and ½ tsp (2.5 mL) baking soda. Store in an airtight container and use within 1 week.

Salt

Salt plays a big role in baking, and omitting it from recipes can lead to mediocre or totally unsuccessful results. Salt enhances the flavor of the other ingredients as well as provides balance and structure. It also acts as a natural preservative. I like to keep the following varieties on hand.

FINE SEA SALT: Fine sea salt is usually my first choice for baking. It doesn't contain iodine or anticaking agents and, unlike iodized table salt, has no bitter aftertaste.

KOSHER SALT: Kosher salt is coarser than sea salt but contains no additives and has a milder flavor than table salt.

FLEUR DE SEL: Fleur de sel is the caviar of salts and should only be used as a finishing salt, such as on top of brownies or lightly sprinkled over caramel sauce.

Sugars, Honey, and Other Sweeteners

Aside from sweetening desserts, sugar acts as a tenderizer in cakes and cookies, prolongs shelf life by helping to retain moisture, and, when used in the right proportions in frozen desserts, will keep them from becoming crystalized.

GRANULATED SUGAR: Granulated or white sugar is the most common type of sugar available and is made from sugar cane or beets and refined to remove all impurities.

SUPERFINE/CASTER SUGAR: Superfine sugar is very finely ground granulated sugar. Because of its fine texture, it dissolves more readily than regular granulated sugar. It's great for making uncooked fruit sauces. Check the label before buying: sometimes cornstarch is added to keep it free-flowing, which can interfere with other ingredients in your recipe. If your superfine sugar clumps, simply sift it before using. To make your own, process granulated sugar in a food processor fitted with the metal blade until very fine.

CONFECTIONERS' SUGAR/POWDERED SUGAR/ICING SUGAR: Confectioners' sugar is granulated sugar that has been very finely granulated to a powdered form. Because it attracts moisture, manufacturers add 3% to 5% cornstarch to keep

it from caking. It is most often used for making icings and frostings and for garnishing.

SANDING SUGAR: Sanding sugar is large, crystallized sugar. Mainly decorative, it is often sprinkled on top of cookies and shortcakes before baking.

GOLDEN/LIGHT BROWN SUGAR: Golden brown sugar is made by adding small quantities of molasses to granulated sugar to give it a slight caramel flavor. It is used in cakes for its subtle caramel flavor and in cookies to impart a soft, chewy texture.

DARK BROWN SUGAR: Dark brown sugar is made the same way as light brown sugar, just with greater quantities of molasses. It has a richer, deeper caramel flavor. If needed, you can substitute demerara sugar for dark brown sugar, as it has a very similar flavor (just be aware that it won't cream as well due to its much coarser granule).

Store all sugars in a cool, dark place. To keep them from hardening, store golden and brown sugars in an airtight container. Adding a slice of apple to the container will help to keep sugar moist.

RAW HONEY: Baked goods made with honey will have a heavier, denser crumb. I always use raw or unpasteurized honey, which has simply been filtered to remove impurities and extend its shelf life, as pasteurized honey can cause an unpleasant aftertaste. I like to keep a neutral-flavored honey, such as clover honey, on hand as well as lavender or chestnut honey for a change in flavor.

CORN SYRUP: Corn syrup is an artificial sweetener derived from cornstarch. When added to syrups and frostings, it helps to keep their texture smooth. It is also often used in candy making.

MOLASSES: Molasses is a byproduct of the sugar-refining process. It's removed from the raw cane sugar juice or beet juice during processing and then is boiled down to concentrate its flavor and color. Because of their superior flavor, dark or blackstrap molasses are best for baking. If you can find them unsulfured, even better.

Chocolate

Scads of books have been written about chocolate, so I won't get carried away here. What you need to know is that using high-quality chocolate is essential to the success of your chocolate desserts. My recipes call for either bittersweet chocolate (70% cocoa content is ideal, but anything higher than 54% will give you excellent results) or semisweet chocolate. These days it is fairly easy to buy good-quality chocolate in your grocery store (Callebaut or Lindt are the most available), but if you can find it, purchase Valrhona (my personal favorite). Specialty stores and chocolate shops sometimes sell it in bulk.

Chocolate will keep for up to 2 years if it is well wrapped and stored in a cool (about 65°F/18°C), dark place. It's a little like wine: it doesn't keep well if the temperature fluctuates greatly.

Here's a handy tip if you find yourself without chocolate (this would never happen to me as I always have several emergency stashes): in some recipes you can substitute cocoa powder for chocolate. Combine 1 tbsp (15 mL) unsalted butter or oil and 3 tbsp (45 mL) cocoa for every 1 ounce (30 g) chocolate called for in a recipe. I would not do this for recipes that contain little or no flour.

Unsweetened Cocoa Powder

Unsweetened cocoa powder comes in two forms: natural cocoa powder and Dutch-process (or alkalized) cocoa powder.

NATURAL COCOA POWDER: Natural cocoa powder is produced from very finely ground roasted cocoa beans. It is dark brown, naturally bitter, with an intense chocolate flavor. It is good for making brownies and simple chocolate cakes.

DUTCH-PROCESS COCOA POWDER: Dutch-process cocoa powder has been treated with an alkaline solution to reduce its natural acidity and make it less bitter tasting. It is reddish and has a mellower flavor than natural cocoa. Dutch-process cocoa is best used in custards, sauces, and icings where you are looking for a more delicate flavor.

Natural cocoa powder is generally paired with baking soda (which is alkali) in recipes. Dutch-process cocoa powder is often used with baking powder. It's important to follow the recipe and not swap one for the other.

Vanilla

I consider vanilla the workhorse flavor maker of the dessert kitchen. Vanilla beans are actually the seedpods of an orchid plant. They are commercially available in three varieties: Tahitian, Madagascar, and Mexican, all distinctly flavored.

PURE VANILLA EXTRACT: Pure vanilla extract is made by macerating the beans in a neutral alcohol for 3 to 4 months. It is indispensible in so many baked goods—cookies, cakes, and pies wouldn't be the same without it. Never buy artificial vanilla; it is 100% chemicals and bears no resemblance to the real thing.

VANILLA BEANS: Choose plump, tender, almost moist-looking vanilla beans—these are fresher and will yield superior flavor. Store vanilla beans in an airtight container for up to 1 year. To use, slice them open lengthwise using a sharp knife and use the tip of the knife to scrape out the tiny black seeds. Don't throw away the pod! You can use it to flavor creams, custards, and sauces or add it to a canister of sugar to make your own vanilla sugar.

spices

The quality and freshness of your spices can have a huge effect on flavor. Purchase spices in small quantities so you can use them up faster, and store them in small airtight containers away from heat and light. I like to keep the following spices in my cupboard, and grind the whole spices as needed using a clean coffee grinder or kitchen rasp.

- allspice, whole
- anise, whole
- cardamon, whole
- cinnamon, whole (preferably Ceylon cinnamon)
- cloves, whole
- ginger, ground
- nutmeg, whole
- star anise, whole

Nuts

All nuts contain oils that can and will make them go rancid if not stored properly. Ideally, store nuts in an airtight container in the refrigerator for up to 3 months and in the freezer for up to 1 year. At a minimum, keep them in a cool, dark place. I like to have the following on hand.

- almonds, whole blanched, slivered, flaked
- hazelnuts/filberts
- macadamia nuts
- pecans
- pine nuts
- pistachios
- walnuts

Almond Paste

Almond paste is available in bakeries and specialty stores, particularly during the holiday season. You can also make your own (see page 319).

Dried Fruit

For best flavor, look for plump, soft dried fruits. Sun-dried varieties are best. Store dried fruit in airtight containers in a cool to cold place. Stored in a cold cellar or refrigerator, they will last for up to 1 year. I like to keep the following unsweetened dried fruit on hand.

- apricots
- cranberries
- figs
- golden raisins
- Medjool dates
- plums
- sultanas
- tart cherries

fridge

Milk Products

- whole/ homogenized milk
- 1% and 2% milk
- buttermilk
- heavy or whipping (35%) cream
- crème fraîche
- plain Greek yogurt
- sour cream

Unsalted Butter

The queen of the dessert kitchen is often imitated but never equaled. When it comes to the dessert kitchen, I only use unsalted butter. I prefer the flavor and being able to control the amount of salt I use in recipes. (The amount of salt added to salted butter can vary greatly, from 1% to 3%.) I also believe unsalted butter is fresher. Dairies often use the freshest milk to make unsalted butter. The salt added to salted butter acts as a preservative and prolongs its shelf life. That being said, there are big differences in quality between the brands available in stores. The moisture content and the diet of the cow will affect how butter tastes and reacts in baking. Experiment with the different brands available to you to see what gives you the best results.

Store butter well wrapped in foil in the refrigerator for up to 3 months or in the freezer for up to 1 year. Changes in light and temperature will affect its shelf life and taste.

Large Free-Range Organic Eggs

All of the recipes in this book call for large free-range organic eggs. I always get the best results using these.

If you buy eggs directly from the farm, refrigerate them and then wash them just before you use them (they have a natural coating that helps to keep them fresher longer). Fresh eggs will keep for up to 1 month in the fridge.

It is easiest to separate eggs when they are cold. If making cookies and cakes, bringing eggs to room temperature before using will give you much greater volume.

Do not use store-bought egg whites to make meringues. Due to the additives, you won't achieve the same volume as egg whites you have separated yourself. You can keep egg whites you have separated yourself in the refrigerator for up to 1 week or in the freezer for up to 3 months.

Fresh Fruit

Buy local, seasonal fresh produce for the best, most flavorful results.

tools & equipment

The following is a list of tools and equipment that I think a well-stocked home baker should have in his or her kitchen. Of course, there are all kinds of other gadgets with very specific purposes you might personally find useful—for example, a cherry pitter would be handy if you plan on making a lot of cherry desserts—but this is a list of my essential items. (Restaurant supply stores have a great selection of quality items at reasonable prices.)

tools

PASTRY BRUSHES: Two natural-bristle pastry brushes: small and medium. Essential for egg or milk washes on pastry.

KITCHEN SCISSORS: Sharp, rustproof scissors with rubber handles.

KNIVES: Assorted types and sizes: bread knife, 8-inch (20 cm) chef's knife, paring knife.

SLOTTED SPOON: Stainless steel: medium.

WOODEN SPOONS: Small, medium, and large.

LADLES: Stainless steel: small, medium, and large.

ICE-CREAM SCOOP: Small and medium (not just for ice cream and sorbet, but also for scooping cookie dough).

WIRE WHISKS
- *Balloon whisk*: one 5- to 6-inch (12.5 to 15 cm) whisk and one 10- to 11-inch (25 to 28 cm) whisk.
- *Sauce whisk*: 8-inch (20 cm).

RUBBER SPATULAS: Heat-resistant rubber spatulas: small, medium, and large.

METAL SPATULAS: Assorted sizes: small, medium, and large, plus one small offset spatula (bent just below the handle).

TONGS: A variety: mini tongs and small, medium, and large tongs (I prefer rubber tips and handles).

MELON BALLER: Aside from scooping melon balls, a melon baller is handy for coring apples and pears.

VEGETABLE PEELER: Buy one that has a sharp edge and feels comfortable in your hand.

CITRUS ZESTER: A small tool the size of a vegetable peeler with 5 small holes at the end to zest citrus fruit.

KITCHEN RASP: A very fine grater for grating spices and chocolate and zesting citrus.

NUTMEG GRATER: Nothing fancy needed. I prefer the type with the lid on the top that allows you to store 1 or 2 nutmegs inside.

FINE-MESH SIEVES: Stainless steel: small, medium, and large.

MEASURING SPOONS: Two sets of stainless steel measuring spoons that run from ⅛ tsp (0.5 mL) to 1 tbsp (15 mL).

MEASURING CUPS: Two sets: one glass or plastic set for liquid measurements and one metal or plastic set for dry measurements.

STAINLESS STEEL MIXING BOWLS: Assorted sizes: a minimum of 5. They are stackable, easy to clean, and last forever.

ROLLING PIN: There are so many types of rolling pins available: tapered at either end or with handles, made of marble, stainless steel, or glass (my mother had a glass rolling pin she could fill with ice and water to keep the pastry cool as she rolled it). My personal preference is a solid, straight, heavy boxwood pin (about 18 inches/46 cm). Find one that suits you.

PASTRY BAGS AND TIPS
· *Pastry bag:* one or two 10- to 12-inch (25 to 30 cm) nylon- or plastic-coated canvas bags for decorating or piping meringues, choux puffs, and truffles. (My favorite are thin nylon pastry bags from France; not easy to come by, but so flexible and easy to control.)
· *Pastry tips:* plain (small ¼ inch/0.5 cm, medium ½ inch/1 cm, and large ¾ inch/2 cm) and star (½ inch/1 cm and ¾ inch/2 cm).

PASTRY BLENDER OR CUTTER: Stainless steel, for blending flour and fat together when making pastry.

PASTRY SCRAPER: Metal with a metal or wooden handle across the top, used to divide dough into smaller portions and to scrape the dough off the counter. Plastic scrapers are very handy for scraping doughs and batters out of bowls.

COOKIE CUTTERS: Assorted shapes and sizes. These also come plain or fluted: I prefer fluted for ascetic reasons. I also like to have various sizes of star- and heart-shaped cutters for making decorative toppings for cobblers and shortcakes.

PARCHMENT PAPER: Cuts easily to fit any pan and makes sticking baked goods a thing of the past.

SILPAT OR NONSTICK LINERS: Rubberized silicone sheet liners can be washed and used over and over again.

pans

BAKING SHEETS: The heavier baking sheets are, the more evenly things cook and the less likely the pans are to warp: two 16- by 14-inch (40 by 35 cm) sheets and two 13- by 10-inch (33 by 25 cm) sheets.

SHEET PANS/JELLY ROLL PANS: The heavier they are, the more evenly things cook and the less likely the pans are to warp: one or two 15½- by 10½- by 1-inch (39 by 26 by 2.5 cm) sheets.

CAKE PANS: Aluminum is the best material for even cooking: two 7-inch (18 cm) pans and two 9-inch (23 cm) pans.

SPRINGFORM PANS: Heavy-gauge aluminum: one 7-inch (18 cm) pan and one 9-inch (23 cm) pan.

LOAF PANS: Aluminum: two 9- by 5- by 3-inch (23 by 12.5 by 7.5 cm) pans. I use them for making semifreddos as well as loaves, and inevitably one is in the freezer. Mini loaf pans are also kind of fun.

RECTANGULAR BAKING PAN: Nonstick light-colored or glass: one 13- by 9- by 2-inch (33 by 23 by 5 cm) pan.

SQUARE BAKING PANS: Nonstick light-colored or glass: one or two 8-inch (20 cm) or 9-inch (23 cm) pans.

PIE PLATE: Glass or metal: one 9-inch (23 cm) pan.

FLUTED TART PANS: Tinned steel with removable bottom: one 7-inch (18 cm) pan, one 9-inch (23 cm) pan, and one 11-inch (28 cm) pan.

GRATIN SERVING DISHES: Ceramic or metal, various sizes: one 12-inch (30 cm) dish and one 16-inch (40 cm) dish. Good-quality dishes bake more evenly and last longer. These are perfect for making bread puddings, cobblers, and crisps.

RAMEKINS: Porcelain: eight to twelve ½ cup (125 mL) ramekins. Useful for crème brûlée, pannacotta, and personal serving-size desserts (handy for dinner parties!).

SAUCEPANS: When it comes to pots and pans, it pays to remember that in most cases you get what you pay for. Beware of packaged sets that are often on sale. Consider what is included (often there are several pots that you will rarely use). Do your homework and remember that this is an investment in your cooking future. Heavy-bottomed nonreactive saucepans are essential for even heating. Copper or aluminum pans are the best conductors of heat, but stainless steel when combined with either of them can be a good solution. Copper pots lined with stainless steel are expensive, high maintenance, and heavy, but will last several lifetimes and are a dream when making any delicate sauce or egg dish. Anodized aluminum pans are nonreactive and very popular right now.

equipment

SCALE: Every serious baker will tell you: weight measurements are much more accurate than volume measurements. A digital scale is a good investment.

THERMOMETERS
- *Candy thermometer:* Necessary for cooking sugar to precise temperatures (for making caramel, for example).
- *Instant-read thermometer:* A good all-purpose thermometer for baking and cooking.
- *Oven thermometer:* Can be very useful for learning how the temperature in your oven behaves.

COOLING RACKS : Two racks: rectangular with a fine wire grid that won't allow cookies to fall through.

HAND-HELD MIXER: If you whip cream or want to make a small batch of anything, an electric hand mixer is handy. Buy a decent-quality one so it lasts.

STAND MIXER: Although you can get away without one, having a stand mixer makes baking and preparing desserts so much easier and way more fun. Choose a good-quality heavy-duty electric stand mixer with a 4- to 5-quart (4 to 5 L) bowl.

FOOD PROCESSOR: A food processor makes quick work of blending pastry and chopping nuts.

MANDOLINE: Japanese versions are versatile and durable for slicing fruit (also useful for vegetable preparation).

JUICER: Unless you plan on making a lot of juice or have citrus trees in your backyard, you won't have need of an electric juicer for baking. My workhorse juicer is a heavy hand-held hinged metal juicer that looks like a giant garlic press.

It is fantastic for juicing lemons, limes, and oranges and keeps most of the seeds from falling into the juice. A wooden citrus reamer is also quick and clean, but you have to watch out for pits in your juice.

ICE-CREAM MAKER: It may seem like an extravagance, but if you want to make ice cream at home, an ice-cream maker is essential. There are a number of excellent models on the market. Buy the best you can afford.

cookies

for best results

Who isn't crazy about homemade cookies? From thin and crunchy to thick, gooey, and chewy, in this chapter I've included a recipe to match every craving. The trick to making irresistible cookies is not skimping on the quality of the ingredients and not overcooking them. Baking them just 1 minute too long can transform a sublime cookie to a merely good cookie. Follow the rest of the tips below and you'll soon be known as a cookie-baking superstar.

01 · For best results, follow the recipe. I have made suggestions where ingredient substitutions make sense, and small tweaks to dried fruits or nuts, for example, will probably be fine. However, I strongly discourage you from substituting the base ingredients. Substituting margarine or vegetable shortening for butter won't yield the same results. If you don't have any butter, try another recipe.

02 · Be careful to measure accurately and consistently follow either the Imperial or metric measures throughout the recipe.

03 · Bring ingredients to room temperature before starting— especially the butter. It will yield better volume and mix faster.

04 · Allow most cookie doughs to rest in the refrigerator overnight. The flour will keep absorbing the wet ingredients for hours after they are mixed, resulting in a denser, moister cookie.

05 · Never put your dough onto a warm baking sheet. Either invest in two or three baking sheets or rinse the sheet under cold running water to cool it off between batches.

06 · For consistent sizing and professional presentation, use an ice-cream scoop to portion the dough onto a lined baking sheet.

07 · Freeze unbaked cookies on the baking sheet. Once frozen, transfer them to an airtight container so you can pull out exactly what you need when you have guests—or a craving! Just set them aside to thaw before baking (it doesn't take long).

lemon clove cookies

makes 3½ dozen cookies

The brightness of lemon marries perfectly with the warmth of cloves in these simple—yet delicious—icebox cookies. You'll find that the cloves in these cookies add a touch of warmth to whatever you pair them with, which makes them perfect companions for sorbet or ice cream (see pages 230–233).

2⅓ cups	all-purpose flour	575 mL
¼ tsp	ground cloves	1 mL
Pinch	fine sea salt	Pinch
1 cup	unsalted butter	250 mL
¾ cup	granulated sugar	175 mL
1	large free-range egg	1
1 tbsp	lemon zest	15 mL
1 tsp	pure vanilla extract	5 mL

1. Preheat oven to 325°F (160°C). Line 2 baking sheets with parchment paper.
2. In a large bowl, combine flour, cloves, and salt. Set aside.
3. In a mixing bowl, using an electric mixer on medium-high speed, cream butter and sugar until light and fluffy. Add egg, zest, and vanilla and mix until well combined. Gradually add dry ingredients to wet ingredients and mix until just combined.
4. Divide dough in half and form each half into a log approximately 2 inches (5 cm) in diameter. Wrap in parchment paper or plastic wrap and refrigerate for at least 2 hours.
5. Remove chilled dough from refrigerator. Slice into ¼-inch (0.5 cm) thick rounds and place on prepared baking sheets, spaced about 1½ inches (4 cm) apart. Bake in preheated oven for 12 to 14 minutes, or until barely golden in color. Remove from oven and cool on baking sheets for 3 to 5 minutes before turning out onto a wire rack to cool completely.

tip

As its name suggests, icebox cookie dough can be made ahead and frozen for up to 1 month (wrap with plastic wrap and overwrap with aluminum foil before freezing). Then simply slice off whatever amount of cookies you'd like and bake from frozen.

variations

You can replace the lemon zest with an equal amount of lime or orange zest. If using lime zest, replace the ground cloves with ground cardamom. If using orange zest, replace the ground cloves with ground cinnamon.

Lemon Clove Cookies (this page) and *Lime Pecan Thins* (page 20)

lime pecan thins

makes 4 dozen cookies

These icebox cookies are more wafers than cookies—light but chewy—with a distinctive nutty and citrusy flavor. Unlike other icebox cookies, they do spread out a bit when they bake, so their shape is slightly rustic. Serve alongside raspberry sorbet or other tart frozen dessert.

1½ cups	unsalted butter	375 mL
2 cups	confectioners' (icing) sugar	500 mL
4 tsp	pure vanilla extract	20 mL
1 tsp	lime oil (see Tip)	5 mL
2 cups	all-purpose flour	500 mL
¼ cup	pecans, toasted and ground	60 mL

tip

Lime oil is available in specialty food stores or online. It keeps for months in your fridge. You could substitute a heaping 2 tsp (10 mL) of finely grated lime zest.

1. Preheat oven to 325°F (160°C). Line 2 baking sheets with parchment paper.
2. In a mixing bowl, using an electric mixer on medium-high speed, cream butter, sugar, vanilla, and lime oil until light and fluffy. Add flour and pecans and mix until well combined. Divide the dough into 3 equal portions and roll each into a log about 1 inch (2.5 cm) in diameter. Wrap each log in parchment paper or plastic wrap. Refrigerate for at least 2 hours (or no longer than 1 week).
3. Remove chilled dough from refrigerator. Slice each roll into ¼-inch (0.5 cm) rounds and place on prepared baking sheets, spaced about 1½ inches (4 cm) apart. Bake in preheated oven for 12 to 15 minutes, or until edges are golden. Remove from oven and cool on baking sheets for 3 to 5 minutes before turning out onto a wire rack to cool completely. These are delicate cookies so be careful moving and storing them.

oatmeal milk-chocolate chunk cookies

makes 3 dozen cookies

Crispy on the outside, chewy on the inside, and laden with the creamy sweetness of milk chocolate—you're sure to get regular requests for these delicious, chunky cookies.

2 cups	all-purpose flour	500 mL
2 cups	old-fashioned rolled oats	500 mL
1 tsp	fine sea salt	5 mL
½ tsp	baking soda	2.5 mL
1 cup	unsalted butter, melted	250 mL
1 cup	granulated sugar	250 mL
1 cup	packed golden brown sugar	250 mL
2	large free-range eggs	2
24	1-inch (2.5 cm) chunks of good-quality milk chocolate	24

1. Preheat oven to 350°F (180°C). Line 2 baking sheets with parchment paper.
2. In a large bowl, combine flour, oats, salt, and baking soda. Set aside.
3. In a medium mixing bowl, combine melted butter and sugars. Add eggs and mix until well combined. Add dry ingredients and mix until just combined. Cover and refrigerate for at least 1 hour or overnight.
4. Remove chilled dough from refrigerator. Using a small ice-cream scoop or a spoon, drop dough, 1 tbsp (15 mL) at a time, on prepared baking sheets, spaced at least 2 inches (5 cm) apart. Place a chunk of milk chocolate on each cookie, pressing down slightly. Bake in preheated oven for 10 to 12 minutes, or until golden. The cookies should still be soft, as they will keep baking as they cool. Remove from oven. Cool for 5 minutes on baking sheets before transferring to a wire rack to cool completely.

variation

For a slightly different take on these, you can substitute the milk chocolate with an equal amount of white or 70% bittersweet (dark) chocolate.

chewy ginger cookies

makes 3 dozen cookies

Of all the ginger cookies I have ever tasted, these are by far my favorite: crunchy and sugar-crusted on the outside, soft and chewy on the inside. These also have a good amount of spice to them, which I really like (a ginger cookie should, after all, be warming). Try serving them alongside Earl Grey tea.

2¼ cups	all-purpose flour	550 mL
2 tsp	baking soda	10 mL
2 tsp	ground ginger	10 mL
1½ tsp	ground allspice	7 mL
1 tsp	ground cinnamon	5 mL
½ tsp	fine sea salt	2.5 mL
¼ tsp	freshly ground black pepper	1 mL
2 cups	unsalted butter	500 mL
1 cup	granulated sugar	250 mL
½ cup	packed golden brown sugar	125 mL
1	large free-range egg	1
⅓ cup	fancy dark molasses	75 mL
·	Granulated sugar	·

1. Preheat oven to 350°F (180°C). Line 2 baking sheets with parchment paper.
2. In a large bowl, sift together flour, baking soda, ginger, allspice, cinnamon, salt, and pepper. Set aside.
3. In a mixing bowl, using an electric mixer on medium-high speed, cream together the butter and sugars until light and fluffy. Add the egg and molasses and mix until well combined. Gradually add dry ingredients and mix until just combined. Cover and refrigerate for 1 hour or overnight.
4. Shape dough, 1 tbsp (15 mL) at a time, into even balls, rolling and coating each in granulated sugar before placing on prepared baking sheets, spaced at least 1½ inches (4 cm) apart. Flatten slightly. Bake in preheated oven for 10 to 12 minutes, or until evenly dark on the top and slightly wrinkled around the edges. Remove from oven and cool on baking sheets for 3 to 5 minutes before turning out onto a wire rack to cool completely.

tips

These cookies spread a lot when baking, so be sure to space them at least 1½ inches (4 cm) apart.

If you prefer your ginger cookies crispy, just bake them for a minute or two longer.

variation

For an easy, decadent dessert, sandwich a scoop of Salted Caramel Ice Cream (page 232) between two ginger cookies.

apricot ginger cookies

makes 3 dozen cookies

These cookies are a grown-up's version of oatmeal raisin cookies: chewy in texture yet complex in flavor (and sweet enough to keep the kiddies happy, too). If you can find it, using organic crystallized ginger will produce more flavorful results than other processed varieties.

½ cup	chopped dried apricots	125 mL
½ cup	slivered almonds, toasted	125 mL
½ cup	candied ginger, chopped	125 mL
1½ cups	old-fashioned rolled oats	375 mL
1½ cups	all-purpose flour	375 mL
½ tsp	fine sea salt	2.5 mL
¼ tsp	baking soda	1 mL
2 cups	granulated sugar	500 mL
1 cup	unsalted butter, softened	250 mL
2	large free-range eggs	2
1 tsp	pure vanilla extract	5 mL

1. Preheat oven to 350°F (180°C). Line 2 baking sheets with parchment paper.
2. In a medium bowl, combine apricots, almonds, and ginger. Set aside.
3. In a large bowl, combine oats, flour, salt, and baking soda. Set aside.
4. In a mixing bowl, using an electric mixer on medium-high speed, cream sugar and butter until light and fluffy. Add eggs, one at a time, and vanilla, and mix until well combined.
5. Mix one-third of the apricot mixture into the butter mixture, followed by one-third of the flour mixture until combined. Repeat two more times until the remaining apricot and flour mixtures are combined. For best results, cover and refrigerate overnight, or at least until chilled, about 2 hours.
6. Drop dough, 1 tbsp (15 mL) at a time, on prepared baking sheets, spaced about 2 inches (5 cm) apart. Bake in preheated oven for 10 to 15 minutes, or until set and slightly brown. Remove from oven and cool on baking sheets for 5 minutes before turning out onto a wire rack to cool completely.

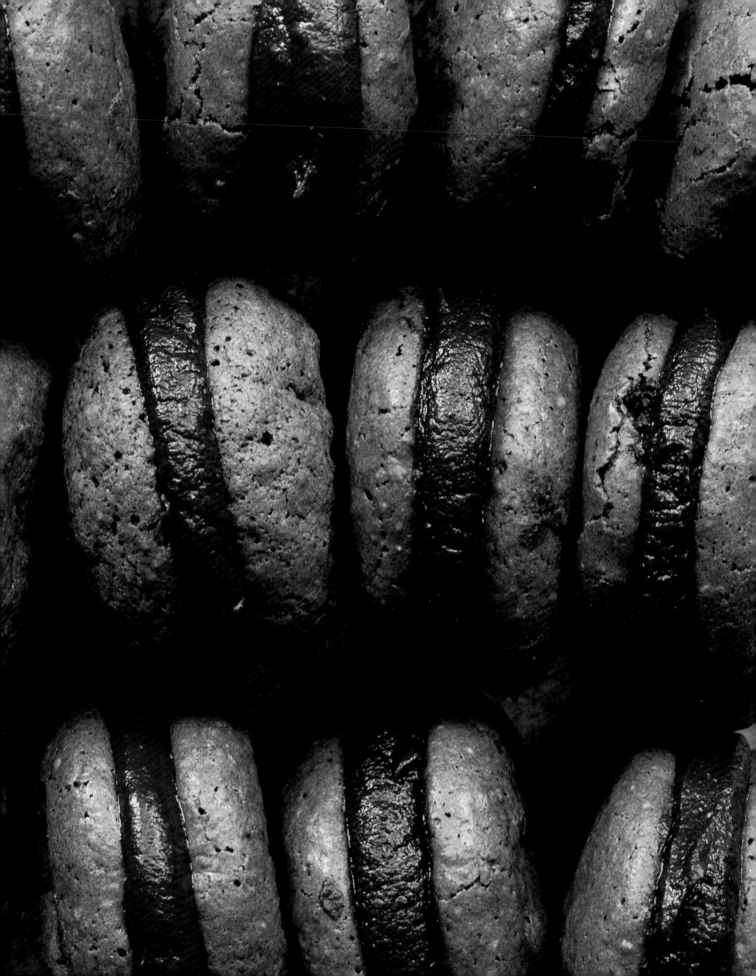

chocolate macarons

makes 2 dozen cookies

Macarons are the quintessential French treat, and they always remind me of my time as a culinary student in Paris. Don't be daunted by the thought of making perfect meringue circles. All you need is a steady hand or, barring that, a series of circular templates drawn out on parchment paper. And if your cookies aren't perfect, that's quite alright— I promise they won't last long once your friends and family find out you've made them.

cookies

1½ cups	whole blanched almonds, toasted and cooled	375 mL
1 cup	confectioners' (icing) sugar	250 mL
4	large free-range egg whites, at room temperature	4
½ cup	granulated sugar	125 mL
⅓ cup	unsweetened cocoa powder	75 mL

ganache

⅓ cup	heavy or whipping (35%) cream	75 mL
2 tbsp	unsalted butter	30 mL
4 oz	70% bittersweet (dark) chocolate, finely chopped	125 mL

1. Preheat oven to 375°F (190°C). Line 2 large baking sheets with parchment paper.
2. MAKE COOKIES: In a food processor fitted with the metal blade, add almonds and confectioners' sugar and pulse until very finely ground. Set aside.
3. In a mixing bowl, using an electric mixer on medium-high speed, beat egg whites until soft peaks form. Sift the cocoa and sugar together, then, about 1 tbsp (15 mL) at a time, gradually add to the egg whites and continue beating until whites are stiff but not dry. Gently fold almond mixture into whites.
4. Place egg whites mixture into a pastry bag fitted with a ½-inch (1 cm) plain tip. Pipe ½-inch (1 cm) rounds onto prepared baking sheets, spaced about ½ inch (1 cm) apart. Bake in preheated oven for 12 minutes, or until just set and slightly deeper in color, exchanging the position of the baking sheets halfway through. Remove from oven and let cool completely on baking sheets.
5. MAKE GANACHE: In a small saucepan over medium heat, bring cream and butter just to boiling point. Remove from heat, add chocolate, then set aside for 3 to 4 minutes, until chocolate is melted. Stir well to combine, then set aside to cool completely.
6. ASSEMBLE: Using a piping bag or spoon, place ganache on the underside of one cookie. Very carefully top with the flat side of a second cookie, gently pressing together to form a sandwich. Repeat with remaining cookies and ganache.

tip

Macarons can be stored in an airtight container at room temperature for a day or two, but if you want to keep them longer, don't add the ganache until the day you are serving them.

variation

Chocolate is traditional, but feel free to get creative with your flavor combinations—I'm a huge fan of caramel and fleur de sel! If you prefer, these macarons can be filled with buttercream (see page 163), but I think that makes them a bit too sweet.

chocolate chip cookies
with caramel chunks

makes 2 dozen cookies

Everyone has an "ultimate" chocolate chip cookie recipe, and this is mine. Adding caramel chunks takes these up a notch and puts a sophisticated twist on this childhood classic. Once you make these I promise they'll be on your go-to list whenever cookies are on the menu. These cookies will stay at their chewy best for several days if kept in an airtight container—if you can keep yourself, and everyone else, from eating them in a single sitting, that is.

1¾ cup	all-purpose flour	425 mL
1 tsp	baking soda	5 mL
1 tsp	fine sea salt	5 mL
1 cup	unsalted butter, softened	250 mL
1¼ cup	packed golden brown sugar	300 mL
½ cup	granulated sugar	125 mL
2	large free-range eggs	2
1 tsp	pure vanilla extract	5 mL
¾ cup	dark chocolate chips	175 mL
¾ cup	Caramel Chunks (optional; see page 76)	175 mL

tip

If you prefer your cookies a bit crispier, just bake these for a couple minutes longer.

1. Preheat oven to 350°F (180°C). Line 2 baking sheets with parchment paper.
2. In a large bowl, sift together flour, baking powder, and salt. Set aside.
3. In a mixing bowl, using an electric mixer on medium-high speed, cream butter and sugars until light and fluffy. Add eggs and vanilla and mix until well combined. Stir in dry ingredients until just combined. Fold in chocolate, and caramel chunks (if using).
4. Using a small ice-cream scoop or a tablespoon, drop dough on prepared baking sheets, spaced about 4 inches (10 cm) apart. Bake in preheated oven for 10 to 12 minutes, or until golden. Remove from oven and cool completely on the baking sheets before serving.

double chocolate espresso cookies

Who needs coffee when you have these? There's enough coffee, dark chocolate, and sugar in these rich and decadent cookies to replace a double shot of espresso (keep these for the adults in your house; they're not meant to be served to children). In fact, make small cookies to serve as an after-dinner pick-me-up and you'll have no need to put a pot of coffee on for your guests (unless it's decaf).

⅓ cup	all-purpose flour	75 mL
1 tsp	espresso powder	5 mL
¾ tsp	baking powder	3 mL
⅛ tsp	fine sea salt	0.5 mL
10 oz	semisweet (65% or higher) chocolate, roughly chopped	300 g
3 tbsp	unsalted butter	45 mL
2 tsp	pure vanilla extract	10 mL
1¼ cups	granulated sugar	300 mL
3	large free-range eggs	3
1 cup	dark chocolate chips	250 mL

1. Preheat oven to 350°F (180°C). Line 2 baking sheets with parchment paper.
2. In a large bowl, sift together flour, espresso powder, baking powder, and salt. Set aside.
3. In a heavy-bottomed saucepan, over low heat, melt chocolate and butter with vanilla. Set aside to cool.
4. Meanwhile, in a mixing bowl, using an electric mixer on medium-high speed, beat sugar and eggs until thickened and light yellow in color. Add the chocolate mixture slowly, stirring all the while until well combined. Add the dry ingredients and stir well. Add chocolate chips, stirring by hand until just combined. The mixture will be very loose. Cover and refrigerate for at least 3 hours or overnight.
5. Working with 1 tbsp (15 mL) of the dough at a time, shape dough into balls and place on prepared baking sheets, spaced at least 3 inches (7.5 cm) apart. Bake in preheated oven for 10 to 12 minutes, or until just set in the middle. Do not overcook. Remove from oven and cool on baking sheets for 3 to 5 minutes before turning out onto a wire rack to cool completely.

tip

Remove these cookies from the oven when the tops become crackly and puff slightly in the center.

reverse white-chocolate chunk cookies

makes 3 dozen cookies

For chocoholics, these cookies are pure perfection: a dreamy combination of bittersweet dough and cocoa butter chunks. Unlike traditional chocolate chunk cookies that mix the chips right into the batter, I suggest that you place the white-chocolate chunks individually onto each cookie just before baking. You'll understand why when you taste them.

2 cups	all-purpose flour	500 mL
1 cup	Dutch-process cocoa	250 mL
1 tsp	baking powder	5 mL
½ tsp	fine sea salt	2.5 mL
1 cup	unsalted butter, softened	250 mL
2 cups	packed golden brown sugar	500 mL
2	large free-range eggs	2
1½ tsp	pure vanilla extract	7 mL
12 oz	white chocolate, cut into chunks	375 g

1. Preheat oven to 350°F (180°C). Line 2 baking sheets with parchment paper.
2. In a large bowl, sift together flour, cocoa, baking powder, and salt. Set aside.
3. In a mixing bowl, using an electric mixer on medium-high speed, cream softened butter and sugar until light and fluffy. Add eggs and vanilla and mix until well combined. Gradually add the dry ingredients until well combined. Cover and refrigerate for at least 1 hour or overnight.
4. Remove chilled dough from refrigerator. Using a small ice-cream scoop or a spoon, drop dough, 1 tbsp (15 mL) at a time, on prepared baking sheets, spaced 2 inches (5 cm) apart. Press 3 chunks of chocolate into each cookie, making sure they are almost totally covered with dough. Bake in preheated oven for 10 to 15 minutes, or until firm on the edges but still soft in the center. Remove from oven and cool on baking sheets for 3 to 5 minutes before turning out onto a wire rack to cool completely.

Reverse White-Chocolate Chunk Cookies (this page) and *Oatmeal Milk-Chocolate Chunk Cookies* (page 21)

white-chocolate hazelnut cookies

makes 3 dozen cookies

People often steer away from recipes with white chocolate, expecting them to be cloyingly sweet. Not so with this cookie! Here the white chocolate imparts a lovely, light sweetness and texture. Sophisticated, delicate, and perfect for any occasion, these are my favorite cookies to serve at an afternoon tea or as an after-dinner nibble alongside a cup of dark espresso or ice wine. I love the chocolate and hazelnut combination, but macadamia nuts or pistachios also work really well.

2½ cups	all-purpose flour	625 mL
½ cup	cornstarch	125 mL
½ tsp	fine sea salt	2.5 mL
2 cups	unsalted butter, softened	500 mL
2 cups	granulated sugar	500 mL
1	large free-range egg	1
½ lb	white chocolate, melted and cooled (see Tip)	250 g
1 tbsp	pure vanilla extract	15 mL
1½ cups	whole hazelnuts, toasted	375 mL
·	Confectioners' (icing) sugar	·

1. Preheat oven to 325°F (160°C). Line 2 baking sheets with parchment paper.
2. In a large bowl, sift together flour, cornstarch, and salt. Set aside.
3. In a mixing bowl, using an electric mixer on medium-high speed, cream butter until light and fluffy. Add sugar and mix until well combined. While mixing, add egg and combine. Add cooled, melted chocolate and vanilla and mix until well combined. Add dry ingredients and mix until well combined. Add hazelnuts and mix until just combined.
4. Shape dough, a scant 1 tbsp (15 mL) at a time, into even balls, rolling and coating each in confectioners' sugar before placing on prepared baking sheets, spaced 2 inches (5 cm) apart. Bake in preheated oven for 8 to 10 minutes, or until edges are golden. Remove from oven and cool on baking sheets for 5 minutes before transferring to a wire rack to cool completely. These are delicate cookies so be careful moving and storing them.

tip

Do not let the melted chocolate cool for longer than about 1 hour. You want it to cool just to room temperature, not to solidify again.

variation

You can substitute an equal amount of macadamia nut halves, pine nuts, or almonds for the hazelnuts.

Pumpkin
Pecan
Thumbprint
Cookies
(page 40)

pumpkin pecan thumbprint cookies

makes 4 dozen cookies

I am a fan of all things pumpkin, so these cookies are a fall favorite when the gourds are plump and plentiful. They're also a perfect way to use up that bit of pumpkin purée left over after the Thanksgiving pies are made. These cookies have become a holiday tradition in our home. This recipe doubles well and produces a ton of cookies, so you can bake them ahead and quickly fill whenever company pops by—a delicious way to spread some holiday cheer.

cookies

2 cups	all-purpose flour	500 mL
1 tsp	baking powder	5 mL
½ tsp	baking soda	2.5 mL
½ tsp	fine sea salt	2.5 mL
1 tsp	ground cinnamon	5 mL
½ tsp	ground nutmeg	2.5 mL
¼ tsp	ground cloves	1 mL
1 cup	old-fashioned rolled oats	250 mL
⅔ cup	unsalted butter	150 mL
½ cup	granulated sugar	125 mL
½ cup	packed golden brown sugar	125 mL
2	large free-range eggs	2
1¼ cups	unsweetened pure pumpkin purée	300 mL
1 tsp	pure vanilla extract	5 mL
1 cup	chopped pitted dates	250 mL
⅓ cup	chopped pecan halves	75 mL

filling

1 cup	cream cheese, at room temperature	250 mL
⅓ cup	packed golden brown sugar	75 mL
⅓ cup	unsweetened pure pumpkin purée	75 mL
1 tsp	ground cinnamon	5 mL
½ cup	chopped pecans	125 mL
48	pecan halves, toasted	48

1. Preheat oven to 350°F (180°C). Line 2 baking sheets with parchment paper.
2. MAKE COOKIES: In a large bowl, sift together flour, baking powder, baking soda, salt, cinnamon, nutmeg, and cloves. Stir in oats. Set aside.
3. In a mixing bowl, using an electric mixer on medium-high speed, cream butter and sugars until light and fluffy. Add eggs, pumpkin, and vanilla and mix until well combined. Mix in dates and pecans. Add dry ingredients and mix until just combined (the dough will be quite stiff).
4. With damp hands, 1 tbsp (15 mL) at a time, roll dough into even balls and place on prepared baking sheets, spaced about 2 inches (5 cm) apart. Using your thumb or the end of a wooden spoon, gently press a well into the center of each cookie. Bake in preheated oven for 8 to 10 minutes, or until just set and slightly golden. Remove from oven and cool on baking sheets for 5 minutes before turning out onto a wire rack to cool completely.
5. MAKE FILLING: Meanwhile, in a clean mixing bowl, using an electric mixer on low speed, mix together cream cheese, brown sugar, pumpkin, and cinnamon just until smooth. Stir in pecans. Cover and refrigerate until chilled, about 2 hours.
6. ASSEMBLE: Spoon chilled pumpkin mixture into a pastry bag fitted with a star tip or a resealable bag with the tip snipped off. Pipe filling into the well of each cooled cookie. Gently press a pecan half into the top of each cookie. Serve immediately or cover and refrigerate for up to 6 hours. (Unfilled cookies will last up to 1 week in an airtight container at room temperature.)

variation

Make candied pecans: Toss pecan halves in caramel sauce (page 305) then arrange in a single layer on a sheet of parchment paper to dry before placing on the cookies.

peanut butter cookies

makes 4 dozen cookies

The trick to peanut butter cookie perfection is all in the baking time. They need to be removed from the oven when they are slightly undercooked (not raw) and perfectly soft. Because of their high fat content, they will continue to cook for quite a while after being removed from the oven. This recipe yields creamy, rich cookies with the perfect level of sweetness.

2½ cups	all-purpose flour	625 mL
½ tsp	baking soda	2.5 mL
½ tsp	fine sea salt	2.5 mL
1½ cups	unsalted butter, softened	375 mL
1 cup	packed golden brown sugar	250 mL
1 cup	granulated sugar	250 mL
1½ cups	natural, salted chunky peanut butter	375 mL
2	large free-range eggs	2
1 tsp	pure vanilla extract	5 mL

1. Preheat oven to 325°F (160°C). Line 2 baking sheets with parchment paper.
2. In a large bowl, sift together flour, baking soda, and salt. Set aside.
3. In a mixing bowl, using an electric mixer on medium-high speed, cream butter and sugars until light and fluffy. Add peanut butter and mix until well combined. Add eggs and vanilla and mix until well combined. Add dry ingredients and mix until just combined. Cover and refrigerate for at least 2 hours or overnight.
4. Remove chilled dough from refrigerator. Using a small ice-cream scoop or a spoon, drop dough, 1 tbsp (15 mL) at a time, on prepared baking sheets, spaced 2 inches (5 cm) apart. Bake in preheated oven for 10 to 12 minutes, or until lightly golden around the edges but still soft in the center. Remove from oven and cool on baking sheets for 3 to 5 minutes before transferring to a wire rack to cool completely.

variation

Chocolate fans can fold in 1½ cups (375 mL) dark chocolate chips in step 3 before refrigerating.

oatmeal raisin cookies

These cookies are dead easy and are my absolute favorite to bake with kids. You don't need to cream the butter; just melt it, add all of the other ingredients, and stir. If you want to shake it up a bit, change the dried fruit: dried cranberries, chunks of dried apricots, even dried pineapple make for a tasty and surprising twist on an old classic.

2 cups	all-purpose flour	500 mL
1 tsp	baking powder	5 mL
1 tsp	baking soda	5 mL
½ tsp	fine sea salt	2.5 mL
2 cups	old-fashioned rolled oats	500 mL
1 cup	salted butter, melted	250 mL
1 cup	granulated sugar	250 mL
1 cup	packed golden brown sugar	250 mL
2	large free-range eggs, at room temperature	2
1 tsp	pure vanilla extract	5 mL
1 cup	Thompson raisins	250 mL

variation

Substitute the raisins with an equal amount of finely chopped dried apricots and 2 tsp (10 mL) finely grated lemon zest.

1. In a medium bowl, sift together flour, baking powder, baking soda, and salt. Stir in oats. Set aside.
2. In a separate large bowl, whisk together melted butter and sugars until well combined. Whisk in eggs and vanilla until well combined. Stir in dry ingredients and mix until just combined. Stir in raisins. Cover and refrigerate for 1 hour or overnight.
3. Preheat oven to 350°F (180°C). Line 2 baking sheets with parchment paper.
4. Remove chilled dough from refrigerator. Using a small ice-cream scoop, drop dough, 1 tbsp (15 mL) at a time, on prepared baking sheets, spaced about 2 inches (5 cm) apart. Bake in preheated oven for 10 to 15 minutes, or until slightly golden around the edges. Remove from oven and cool on baking sheets for 3 to 5 minutes before turning out onto a wire rack to cool completely.

variations

Feel free to change the type of nuts you use; hazelnuts, Brazil nuts, and walnuts all work here. You can substitute the apricots and cranberries with dried pineapple, dried cherries, or dried apples.

winterfruit drops

makes 3 dozen cookies

My mother's friend Aggie gave me a variation of this recipe years ago, and it has since become a staple in my pantry during the winter months. These cookies are moist and chewy, and the dried fruit—especially the dates—provide a nice amount of natural sweetness. Make this recipe your own by substituting your favorite fruits and nuts.

4 cups	lightly packed pitted Medjool dates, quartered	1 L
1 cup	dried apricots	250 mL
1 cup	dried cranberries or blueberries	250 mL
1 cup	pecan halves, toasted	250 mL
1 cup	slivered almonds, toasted	250 mL
1⅓ cups	all-purpose flour, divided	325 mL
¾ tsp	baking soda	3 mL
½ tsp	fine sea salt	2.5 mL
¾ tsp	ground cinnamon	3 mL
⅛ tsp	ground nutmeg	0.5 mL
¾ cup	unsalted butter, softened	175 mL
1 cup	packed golden brown sugar	250 mL
2	large free-range eggs	2
½ tsp	pure vanilla extract	2.5 mL

1. Preheat oven to 350°F (180°C). Line 2 baking sheets with parchment paper.
2. In a large bowl, combine dates, apricots, cranberries, pecans, almonds, and ⅓ cup (75 mL) of the flour. Set aside.
3. In a separate bowl, sift together remaining 1 cup (250 mL) flour, baking soda, salt, cinnamon, and nutmeg. Set aside.
4. In a mixing bowl, using an electric mixer on medium-high speed, cream butter and sugar until light and fluffy. Add eggs and vanilla and mix until well combined. Add dry ingredients and mix until just combined. Add dried fruit and nuts and, because this mixture is stiff, use your hands to combine the ingredients well.
5. Drop dough, a heaping 1 tbsp (15 mL) at a time, on prepared baking sheets, spaced about 2 inches (5 cm) apart. Bake in preheated oven for 8 to 10 minutes, or until slightly golden but still soft. Remove from oven and cool on baking sheets for 5 minutes before turning out onto a wire rack to cool completely.

The Reserve Power Cookies (page 48)
and *Winterfruit Drops* (this page)

tips

Change the combination of fruit and nuts depending on your tastes and what you have on hand, but don't remove the dates—they are a key ingredient needed to help bind and sweeten this cookie.

The quality of the dates used in this recipe is important: look for Medjool dates (do not buy dried pitted pressed dates that are sold in blocks in the baking section of most grocery stores). It is worth the extra cost and time to pit them yourself.

Store in an airtight container at room temperature for up to 1 week (the dried fruit keeps them moist and chewy).

the reserve power cookies

makes 2 dozen large cookies

This recipe came about after several friends from "The Reserve"—a golf community in California—requested a cookie that was easy to pack, super tasty, and contained enough "stuff" to keep them fueled when out on long hikes. Jammed with dried fruit, seeds, and oats, this is the answer. Keep a batch of these on hand for that mid-morning or -afternoon energy boost you might need.

1 cup	whole-wheat flour	250 mL
2 cups	old-fashioned rolled oats	500 mL
½ tsp	baking soda	2.5 mL
1 cup	apricots, cut into slivers	250 mL
½ cup	unsweetened shredded coconut	125 mL
½ cup	bittersweet chocolate chips	125 mL
½ cup	dried tart cherries	125 mL
½ cup	raw walnuts	125 mL
¼ cup	hemp seeds	60 mL
¼ cup	raw unsalted sesame seeds or flaxseeds	60 mL
½ cup	raw unsalted pumpkin seeds	125 mL
1 tsp	ground cinnamon	5 mL
1	large free-range egg, beaten	1
¼ cup	canola oil	60 mL
1 tsp	pure vanilla extract	5 mL
¾ cup	unsweetened applesauce	175 mL
½ cup	lightly packed golden brown sugar	125 mL
½ cup	pure maple syrup	125 mL

tip

Use whatever dried fruit, seeds, or nuts you like and have in your pantry.

1. Preheat oven to 350°F (180°C). Line 2 baking sheets with parchment paper.
2. In a large mixing bowl, combine flour, oats, baking soda, apricots, coconut, chocolate chips, cherries, walnuts, hemp seeds, pumpkin seeds, and cinnamon.
3. In a separate bowl, combine egg, oil, vanilla, applesauce, brown sugar, and maple syrup. Pour the wet ingredients into the dry ingredients and stir until just combined.
4. Scoop dough onto a tablespoon, flatten with a wet hand (this dough is very sticky), then drop onto prepared baking sheets, spaced about 1 inch (2.5 cm) apart. Bake in preheated oven for 12 to 15 minutes, or until firm and golden brown around the edges. Remove from oven and cool on baking sheets for 5 minutes before turning out onto a wire rack to cool completely.

bars & biscotti

for best results

There's something so comforting about a sweet treat served alongside a steaming cup of coffee or tea. A decadent brownie, a gooey butter tart square, or a crunchy chocolate espresso biscotti is perfect for taking an indulgent break with. Bars are also a fantastic dessert to serve a crowd or to wrap up for a weekend away, and they make an easy, elegant dessert when paired with ice cream or fresh fruit. I have included four of my favorite biscotti recipes. Although they are a bit of work, they make good-size batches and keep for ages, making them a brilliant gift for friends.

01 · For best results, follow the recipe. I have made suggestions where ingredient substitutions make sense, and small tweaks to dried fruits or nuts, for example, will probably be fine. However, I strongly discourage you from substituting the base ingredients. Substituting margarine or vegetable shortening for butter won't yield the same results. If you don't have any butter, try another recipe.

02 · Be careful to measure accurately and consistently follow either the Imperial or metric measures throughout the recipe.

03 · Bring ingredients to room temperature before starting—especially the butter. It will yield better volume and mix faster.

04 · When a recipe calls for mixing nuts into a batter, toast the nuts slightly in a dry pan beforehand (and allow to cool before using). The nuts will have a richer, fuller flavor.

05 · When baking bars, line the pans with foil so you can easily remove them from the pan. This also makes cleaning the pan a breeze.

06 · Use a hot, wet knife to cleanly cut bars into squares (hold knife under hot running water to heat).

07 · When baking biscotti (after the first bake), place them cut-side down on the pan and be careful not to overcrowd them. Space them about 1 inch (2.5 cm) apart.

lemon shortbread bars

makes 16 squares

Everyone needs a good lemon bar in their arsenal. This recipe was the result of months spent in my catering kitchen searching for the perfect balance between sweet and tart. I think it hits the mark. The shortbread base, which has a sweet, light, yet firm snap, enhances the flavor of the filling.

	base	
1½ cups	all-purpose flour	375 mL
½ cup	almond flour/meal	125 mL
½ cup	confectioners' (icing) sugar	125 mL
¼ tsp	fine sea salt	1 mL
¾ cup	cold unsalted butter, cut into 1-inch (2.5 cm) cubes	175 mL

	filling	
2½ cups	granulated sugar	625 mL
½ cup	all-purpose flour	125 mL
¼ tsp	fine sea salt	1 mL
6	large free-range eggs	6
1 cup	freshly squeezed lemon juice (juice of about 8 lemons)	250 mL
•	Finely grated zest of 2 lemons	•
•	Confectioners' (icing) sugar	•

1. Preheat oven to 325°F (160°C). Butter a 13- by 9-inch (33 by 23 cm) metal baking pan.
2. MAKE BASE: In a food processor fitted with the metal blade, add flours, confectioners' sugar, and salt and pulse briefly to combine. Scatter the butter cubes over the mixture and pulse until the dough just begins to come together. Crumble the dough into the prepared baking pan and, using your fingers, press evenly over bottom of pan. Bake in preheated oven for about 20 minutes, or until the crust is fully set and just starting to brown at the edges. Remove pan from oven and place on a wire rack to cool.
3. MAKE FILLING: Meanwhile, in a large bowl, combine sugar, flour, salt, and eggs and whisk until the sugar has dissolved and the mixture is smooth, about 2 minutes. Add lemon juice and whisk until well combined.
4. ASSEMBLE: Pour the filling over the baked crust. Bake in preheated oven for 20 to 25 minutes, or until set (the filling should wiggle slightly in the center when gently shaken). Remove pan from the oven and place on wire rack to cool completely. Refrigerate for several hours or until chilled before cutting into bars. Dust with confectioners' sugar before serving.

tips

Use fresh organic lemons as well as good-quality unsalted butter—it really does make all the difference in the world.

Use a hot, wet knife to cleanly cut through the lemon filling (hold knife under hot running water to heat).

You can dress up this dessert by serving it with fresh berries and a scoop of semifreddo (see pages 220–226).

carmelita bars

makes 2 dozen squares

Sweet, chewy oats mixed with dark chocolate and caramel—delicious. These bars will keep for ages in the fridge and also freeze really well, so it's worth making a double batch to have some on hand when a snack attack occurs. They also package easily for lunch boxes or road trips (just remember to separate them with a little parchment paper so that if they get warm, they're still easy to handle).

caramel

¾ cup	unsalted butter	175 mL
½ cup	liquid honey	125 mL
¼ cup	heavy or whipping (35%) cream	60 mL
½ cup	packed golden brown sugar	125 mL

ganache

7½ oz	semisweet chocolate, roughly chopped	225 g
1 cup	heavy or whipping (35%) cream	250 mL
2 tbsp	unsalted butter	30 mL

base and topping

6 cups	old-fashioned rolled oats	1.5 L
½ cup	all-purpose flour	125 mL
1⅓ cups	packed golden brown sugar	325 mL
1 tsp	fine sea salt	5 mL
1⅓ cups	unsalted butter	325 mL
¾ tsp	pure vanilla extract	3 mL

1. MAKE CARAMEL: In a heavy-bottomed saucepan over low heat, bring butter, honey, cream, and sugar to a low boil and simmer for 5 minutes. Remove from heat and cool in saucepan for 15 to 20 minutes.
2. MAKE GANACHE: In a small bowl set over a saucepan of simmering water (make sure water does not touch bottom of bowl), combine chocolate, cream, and butter, stirring continuously until the chocolate has completely melted. Remove top pan from the heat and set aside for 15 minutes to cool.
3. Preheat oven to 350°F (180°C). Line a 13- by 9-inch (33 by 23 cm) metal baking pan with parchment paper.
4. MAKE BASE AND TOPPING: In a large bowl, combine oats, flour, sugar, and salt. Set aside.

continued . . .

5. In a small saucepan over low heat, melt butter and stir in vanilla. Pour over dry ingredients and stir until thoroughly combined. Set aside.

6. FINISH: Press two-thirds of the oat mixture into the bottom of the prepared pan. Bake in preheated oven for 7 minutes, or until lightly golden and firm to the touch.

7. Remove pan from oven and pour caramel over the base. Let stand for 2 to 3 minutes. Drizzle ganache over the caramel-soaked base. Sprinkle remaining base and topping mixture over the ganache and press down very lightly. Bake in preheated oven for 20 minutes, or until lightly golden. Remove from oven and set pan on a wire rack to cool completely. Refrigerate for at least 2 to 3 hours, until firm and chilled. Cut into bars.

tips

You will want to dive into these bars the minute they come out of the oven. Resist! They need to cool completely and firm up, otherwise you will end up with a crumbled—albeit delicious—mess.

Stored in an airtight container, these bars will keep in the refrigerator for up to 1 week or in the freezer for up to 1 month.

charlotte bars

Packed with yummy ingredients, this bar is named after my great-niece, Charlotte, who comes from a family who loves to cook and entertain. You can use whatever dried fruit or nuts you may have on hand and get wonderful results.

1¼ cups	all-purpose flour	300 mL
2 tbsp	espresso powder	30 mL
1½ tsp	baking soda	7 mL
½ tsp	fine sea salt	2.5 mL
½ lb	unsalted butter	250 g
1½ cups	packed golden brown sugar	375 mL
2	large free-range eggs	2
2 tsp	pure vanilla extract	10 mL
¾ cup	old-fashioned rolled oats	175 mL
1 cup	chopped pitted Medjool dates	250 mL
1½ cups	hazelnuts, toasted and roughly chopped	375 mL
1½ cups	chocolate chips (Belgian if you can get them)	375 mL
1½ cups	dried cranberries	375 mL
•	Confectioners' (icing) sugar	•

1. Preheat oven to 350°F (180°C). Butter a 13- by 9-inch (33 by 23 cm) metal baking pan and line with parchment paper.
2. In a medium bowl, sift together flour, espresso, baking soda, and salt. Set aside.
3. In a saucepan over low heat, combine butter and sugar, stirring until butter is melted and sugar is dissolved. Remove from heat, cool slightly, and pour into a large bowl. Add eggs and vanilla and stir until smooth. Add dry ingredients and stir well. Add oats, dates, hazelnuts, chocolate chips, and dried cranberries and stir until well combined. Scrape mixture into prepared pan and, using your fingers, spread evenly over bottom of pan. Bake in preheated oven for 20 to 30 minutes, or until the surface is slightly firm to the touch and the sides have pulled away from the pan. Remove pan from oven and transfer to a wire rack to cool completely. Dust with confectioners' sugar. Cut into bars.

oatmeal almond bars

makes 20 bars

A sweet and crunchy take on homemade granola bars, these are perfect for the lunchbox or a picnic: easy to pack, easy to eat, and yummy enough to be called dessert. Try making them with a mix of nuts or, if you prefer, omit the nuts entirely. For a power-charged pocket snack that will keep you going, include the hemp, flax, or chia seeds.

1 cup	lightly packed golden brown sugar	250 mL
½ cup	unsalted butter, melted	125 mL
1 cup	old-fashioned rolled oats	250 mL
1 tsp	baking soda	5 mL
1 cup	unsweetened flaked coconut	250 mL
½ cup	slivered almonds, toasted	125 mL
1 tbsp	sesame seeds, hemp seeds, or flaxseeds	15 mL
1 tsp	pure vanilla extract	5 mL

1. Preheat oven to 350°F (180°C). Butter a 9-inch (23 cm) square metal baking pan.
2. In a medium mixing bowl, stir together melted butter and sugars. Add oats, baking soda, coconut, nuts, seeds, and vanilla and stir until well combined.
3. Transfer mixture to prepared baking pan and, using your fingers, press evenly over bottom of pan. Bake in preheated oven for 15 minutes, or until golden around the edges. Remove pan from oven and place on wire rack to cool completely. Cut into bars.

variations

01 · Substitute the almonds with an equal amount of toasted chopped pecans, hazelnuts, walnuts, or macadamia nuts.

02 · Add ⅓ cup (75 mL) finely chopped dried fruit (such as apricots and cranberries) in step 2.

03 · Add ½ cup (125 mL) hemp, flaxseeds, or chia seeds in step 2.

Oatmeal Almond Bars (this page)
and *Charlotte Bars* (page 57)

butter tart bars

makes 16 small squares

Who doesn't love butter tarts? They're a quintessential Canadian dessert. The idea for turning them into bars originated with a close family friend who got tired of making individual tarts and instead opted for this deliciously messy, gooey creation—and to be honest, I like them a lot better in bar form. Most people associate butter tarts with the holidays, but these are so good I recommend not waiting until then to try them.

base

1¼ cups	all-purpose flour	300 mL
¼ cup	packed golden brown sugar	60 mL
½ cup	cold unsalted butter, cut into ¼-inch (0.5 cm) cubes	125 mL

filling

1 cup	packed golden brown sugar	250 mL
1 tbsp	all-purpose flour	15 mL
⅓ cup	unsalted butter, melted	75 mL
2 tbsp	heavy or whipping (35%) cream	30 mL
1 tsp	pure vanilla extract	5 mL
1	large free-range egg	1
1 cup	Thompson raisins	250 mL

1. Preheat oven to 350°F (180°C). Butter a 9-inch (23 cm) square metal baking pan.
2. MAKE BASE: In a bowl, combine flour and sugar. Add the butter cubes and, using your fingers, rub the butter into the dry ingredients until the mixture is the consistency of coarse sand. Press mixture firmly into the bottom of prepared baking pan. Bake in preheated oven for 15 minutes, or until slightly golden around the edges. Remove from oven and set aside.
3. MAKE FILLING: Meanwhile, in a small bowl, combine sugar and flour. Set aside.
4. In a mixing bowl, whisk together melted butter, cream, and vanilla. Add egg and whisk until well combined. Stir in dry ingredients. Stir in raisins.
5. ASSEMBLE: Pour filling over base. Bake in preheated oven for 20 to 25 minutes, or until the top springs back when lightly touched. Remove pan from oven and set on wire rack to cool completely. Cut into bars.

tip

Using a hot knife to cut the bars will make the job easier (small squares are better here—these bars are sweet . . . in a good way!).

chocolate raincoast crisp tiffin bars

makes 16 bars

This recipe combines all of my favorite things: dark chocolate, dried fruit, and Raincoast Crisps. When choosing a flavor of crisps for your recipe, I recommend going with one of the fruitier versions: Cranberry and Hazelnut, Rosemary Raisin Pecan, or even Salty Date and Almond. If you need a gluten-/nut-free dessert, grab a box of Cranberry Oat Crisps. Serve with a cup of ginger tea or, for a real pick-me-up, an espresso.

1 package	Rosemary Raisin Pecan or Cranberry and Hazelnut Raincoast Crisps, broken into small pieces	1 package
½ cup	dried cherries or dried cranberries	125 mL
½ cup	hazelnuts or pecans, toasted, coarsely chopped	125 mL
½ cup	golden syrup, golden corn syrup, or liquid honey	125 mL
10 oz	70% bittersweet (dark) chocolate, chopped into small chunks	300 g
7 tbsp	unsalted butter	105 mL

tips

This bar is quite rich, so cut it into small pieces. Long, thin fingers work well.

If you can't find any golden syrup (sold in most shops that carry British staples), you can substitute an equal amount of golden corn syrup without affecting the flavor or texture too much.

1. Line a 9-inch (23 cm) square metal baking pan with parchment paper.
2. In a large bowl, combine crisps, cherries, and hazelnuts. Set aside.
3. In a medium saucepan over low heat, add syrup, chocolate, and butter, stirring until completely melted and well combined. Pour over dry ingredients. Using a wooden spoon, stir well. Scrape mixture evenly into prepared pan, and, using the back of a tablespoon, press evenly to flatten the top. Cool completely, then refrigerate for at least 2 hours until chilled. Cut into bars.

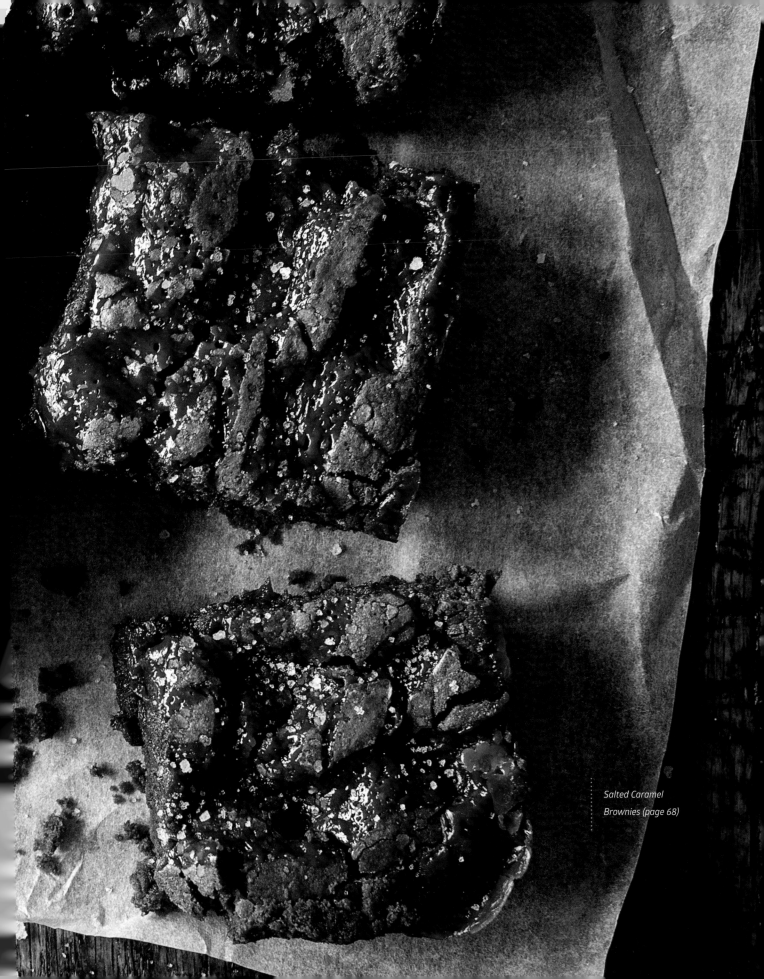

*Salted Caramel
Brownies (page 68)*

salted caramel brownies

The combination of caramel, chocolate, and salt make this an incredibly indulgent brownie, although you can omit the caramel if you really want to. The caramel recipe makes more than you need for the brownies, but it keeps well in the fridge and is fantastic on ice cream or drizzled over fresh fruit. Serve these brownies with Chocolate and Gosling's Rum Semifreddo (page 226). You can go to the gym tomorrow.

caramel

1 cup	granulated sugar	250 mL
¼ cup	water	60 mL
½ cup	heavy or whipping (35%) cream, at room temperature	125 mL

batter

1 cup	unsalted butter	250 mL
8 oz	70% bittersweet (dark) chocolate, chopped into chunks	250 g
4	large free-range eggs	4
1 scant cup	granulated sugar	scant 250 mL
1 scant cup	packed golden brown sugar	scant 250 mL
2 tsp	pure vanilla extract	10 mL
1 cup	all-purpose flour	250 mL
½ tsp	fine sea salt	2.5 mL
½ cup	caramel (recipe above)	125 mL
½ tsp	sea salt flakes	2.5 mL

1. MAKE CARAMEL: In a medium heavy-bottomed saucepan over medium heat, bring sugar and water to a boil. Reduce heat and simmer until mixture starts to turn golden. For more even caramelizing, swirl the mixture in the pan several times. *Do not stir with a spoon at this stage.* Cook until a deep golden color, but watch carefully, as it can burn quickly. Remove from heat and very slowly pour in cream—it will bubble up furiously and then subside. Return saucepan to stove over low heat and stir to combine. Remove from heat and cool to room temperature. Set aside ½ cup (125 mL) to use for this recipe. Refrigerate the rest in an airtight container for another use (it will keep for up to 10 days in the refrigerator or up to 3 months in the freezer).

2. Preheat oven to 325°F (160°C). Butter a 9-inch (23 cm) square metal baking pan.

3. MAKE BATTER: In a medium heavy-bottomed saucepan over low heat, melt butter and chocolate, stirring until smooth. Remove from heat and set aside to cool slightly.

4. In a medium bowl, whisk together eggs, sugars, and vanilla. Add cooled chocolate mixture and whisk to combine. Whisk in flour and salt.

5. FINISH: Pour half of the batter into the prepared pan. Using a tablespoon, spoon ¼ cup (60 mL) of caramel over the batter. Pour in the remaining batter. Spoon the remaining ¼ cup (60 mL) of caramel over the batter. Sprinkle with salt flakes. Bake in preheated oven for 18 to 20 minutes, or until just set. Remove pan from oven and place on a wire rack to cool completely. Cut into squares.

tip

Every oven is different, so you may need to adjust the cooking time to suit your oven. The brownies should be slightly wet inside when you remove them from the oven, as they will continue baking for a few minutes. Be careful not to overcook them: you want to make sure they are ooey-gooey good.

apricot almond biscotti
with white chocolate

makes 5½ biscotti

Unlike most other biscotti, these are not rock hard but have a more cookie-like texture. The recipe is inspired by my hairstylist's mother, Barbara Wheeler, who always sends a box to her daughter's salon during the holidays. This recipe does make a lot, but they keep so well it makes the effort more than worthwhile.

5½ cups	all-purpose flour	1.4 L
5 tsp	baking powder	25 mL
1 tsp	fine sea salt	5 mL
1½ cups	dried apricots, coarsely chopped	375 mL
1½ cups	sliced almonds	375 mL
1 cup	unsalted butter, softened	250 mL
2¼ cups	granulated sugar	560 mL
4	large free-range eggs	4
2 cups	white-chocolate callets, divided	500 mL
½ cup	freshly squeezed orange juice	125 mL

tip

The logs do expand during the first baking so don't crowd them on the baking sheets.

1. Preheat oven to 325°F (160°C). Line a baking sheet with parchment paper.
2. In a large bowl, sift together flour, baking powder, and salt. Add apricots and almonds and toss to combine. Set aside.
3. In a small bowl set over a saucepan of simmering water (make sure water does not touch bottom of bowl), melt 1 cup (250 mL) white chocolate, stirring until smooth. Remove from heat and set aside to cool.
4. In a mixing bowl, using an electric mixer on medium-high speed, cream butter and sugar until light and fluffy. Add eggs and mix until well combined. Add melted white-chocolate and mix to combine, then add remaining 1 cup (250 mL) white-chocolate callets. Add orange juice and mix to combine. Add dry ingredients and mix until just combined.
5. Divide dough into 3 equal portions and, on prepared baking sheet, form into 3 logs, flattening them slightly. Bake in preheated oven for 30 minutes, or until dry, firm, and barely golden. Remove from oven and cool on baking sheets for 5 minutes.
6. Reduce oven temperature to 275°F (140°C).
7. Using a sharp knife, cut the logs into ¾-inch (2 cm) wide diagonal slices. Return slices to baking sheets cut-side down, spaced about 1 inch (2.5 cm) apart. Bake in reduced-temperature oven for 30 to 40 minutes, or until firm. Remove from oven and cool on baking sheets for 5 minutes before turning out onto a wire rack to cool completely. Store in an airtight container in the refrigerator for up to 2 weeks or freeze for up to 3 months.

hazelnut anise biscotti

makes 5 dozen biscotti

You'll find this classic Italian biscotti flavor combination in every café across Rome. The anise flavor is a bit of a surprise to North American palates, and the hazelnut is a lovely, rich savory foil to the inherent sweetness of the seeds. These biscotti make the perfect hostess gift: they package up beautifully and keep well in either the freezer or a good-quality cookie tin.

5¼ cups	all-purpose flour	1.3 L
3¾ tsp	baking powder	18 mL
½ tsp	fine sea salt	2.5 mL
1¼ cups	unsalted butter	300 mL
1¾ cups	granulated sugar	425 mL
5	large free-range eggs	5
1 cup	whole hazelnuts, lightly toasted	250 mL
2 tsp	aniseed	10 mL

1. Preheat oven to 325°F (160°C). Line 2 baking sheets with parchment paper.
2. In a large bowl, sift together flour, baking powder, and salt. Set aside.
3. In a mixing bowl, using an electric mixer on medium-high speed, cream butter and sugar until light and fluffy. Add eggs and vanilla and mix until well combined, making sure to scrape down the sides of the work bowl. Add dry ingredients and mix until just combined. Add hazelnuts and aniseed and mix well.
4. Divide dough into 4 equal portions. On a flat surface, roll into 4 logs. Each log should be about 12 inches (30 cm) long and 3 inches (7.5 cm) in diameter (no wider than that!), and should weigh about 1½ lbs (750 g). Transfer to prepared baking sheets and bake in preheated oven for 30 to 35 minutes, until firm. Remove from oven and cool on baking sheets for 5 minutes.
5. Using a serrated knife, cut the logs into diagonal slices ½ inch (1 cm) wide. Return slices to baking sheet cut-side down. Bake for 20 to 25 minutes, or until lightly golden. Remove from oven and cool on baking sheets for 5 minutes before turning out onto a wire rack to cool completely.

variations

MAKE ORANGE PISTACHIO BISCOTTI: Substitute the hazelnuts with an equal amount of lightly toasted pistachios. Substitute the aniseed with the zest of 2 oranges.

Apricot Almond Biscotti with White Chocolate (page 70), *Hazelnut Anise Biscotti* (page 71), *Chocolate Pecan Rum Biscotti* (page 75), and *Chocolate, Caramel, and Espresso Biscotti* (page 76)

chocolate pecan rum biscotti

makes about 3 dozen biscotti

This biscotti is a bit of a departure from the other biscotti recipes included in this book: it's more akin to a cookie than the original Italian biscuit. We were constantly baking these to keep up with demand at the store. Its deep cocoa flavor and toasty crunch make it a big hit.

7½ oz	70% bittersweet (dark) chocolate	225 g
5 oz	unsalted butter	150 g
2½ cups	all-purpose flour	625 mL
1½ cups	unsweetened cocoa powder	375 mL
1½ tsp	baking powder	7 mL
¾ tsp	fine sea salt	3 mL
5	large free-range eggs	5
1½ cups	granulated sugar	375 mL
1¾ cups	packed golden brown sugar	425 mL
⅓ cup	brewed coffee	75 mL
1 tbsp	medium or dark rum	15 mL
1½ cups	whole pecans, toasted	375 mL

1. Preheat oven to 300°F (150°C). Line a baking sheet with parchment paper.
2. In a small heavy-bottomed saucepan over low heat, melt chocolate and butter, stirring until smooth. Remove from heat and set aside to cool slightly.
3. In a large bowl, sift together flour, cocoa, baking powder, and salt. Set aside.
4. In a mixing bowl, using an electric mixer on medium-high speed, mix eggs and sugars until foamy. Add coffee, rum, and vanilla and mix to combine. Add melted chocolate and mix to combine. Add dry ingredients and nuts and mix until well combined. Cover and refrigerate for at least 2 hours or overnight.
5. Remove chilled dough from refrigerator. Divide dough into 3 equal portions and, on prepared baking sheet, form into 3 logs the length of the pan. Bake in preheated oven on the bottom rack for 50 minutes, or until dry. Remove from oven and cool on baking sheets for 5 minutes.
6. Using a sharp serrated knife, cut the logs into ¼-inch (0.5 cm) wide slices on a slight diagonal. Return slices to baking sheet cut-side down, spaced about 1 inch (2.5 cm) apart. Bake for 5 to 7 minutes, or until firm. Remove from oven and cool on baking sheets for 5 minutes before turning out onto a wire rack to cool completely.

chocolate, caramel, and espresso biscotti

makes 4½ dozen biscotti

This is my favorite biscotti recipe by far and the most popular among my friends and family. The caramel chunks add a delicious buttery flavor and distinctive snap to the texture, while the chocolate and espresso add richness. Unlike most biscotti recipes where you can fit 2 logs per baking sheet, this recipe requires placing only 1 log per sheet, as they spread a bit more than usual due to the sugar and chocolate.

caramel chunks

2 cups	granulated sugar	500 mL
1 cup	water	250 mL

biscotti

4 cups	all-purpose flour	1 L
1½ tsp	baking powder	7 mL
¾ tsp	fine sea salt	3 mL
1 cup	unsalted butter	250 mL
¾ cup	granulated sugar	175 mL
4	large free-range eggs	4
½ tsp	pure vanilla extract	2.5 mL
6½ oz	dark chocolate callets	190 g
6½ oz	Caramel Chunks (recipe above)	190 g
½ cup	water	125 mL
2 tbsp	espresso powder	30 mL

tip

It is hard to tell when these biscotti are done baking (they are already dark in color), so you have to go by touch: the logs should be dry and slightly firm when you take them out of the oven, and the slices should be totally dried out.

1. MAKE CARAMEL CHUNKS: Lightly oil a 13- by 9-inch (33 by 23 cm) metal baking pan.
2. In a heavy-bottomed saucepan, bring sugar and water to a boil, then reduce heat to a simmer. Swirl syrup in pot to even out the cooking, since it will color around the edge first. *Do not use a spoon to do this.* Keep cooking and swirling until the syrup turns dark golden amber in color. Remove pan from the heat.
3. Pour syrup onto prepared baking sheet. Set aside to cool completely. Using a wooden mallet or rolling pin, crack hardened caramel into ½-inch (1 cm) to ¾-inch (2 cm) chunks. Set aside.

4. Preheat oven to 325°F (160°C). Line 2 baking sheets with parchment paper.
5. MAKE BISCOTTI: In a large bowl, sift together flour, baking powder, and salt. Set aside.
6. In a mixing bowl, using an electric mixer on medium-high speed, cream butter and sugar until light and fluffy. Add eggs and vanilla and mix until well combined, making sure to scrape down the side of the work bowl. Add dry ingredients and mix until just combined. Add chocolate, caramel chunks, and espresso powder and mix until just combined.
7. Divide dough into 2 equal portions and, on a flat surface, form into 2 logs. Each log should be about 12 inches (30 cm) long and 3 inches (7.5 cm) in diameter (no wider than that!), and should weigh about 1½ lbs (750 g). Bake in preheated oven for 30 to 35 minutes, until firm. Remove from oven and cool on baking sheets for 5 minutes.
8. Using a sharp serrated knife, cut the logs into diagonal slices ½ inch (1 cm) wide. Return slices to baking sheets cut-side down. Bake for 20 to 25 minutes, or until lightly golden. Remove from oven and cool on baking sheets for 5 minutes before turning out onto a wire rack to cool completely.

tarts &
more tarts

for best results

I can't deny it: I love pastry. Shortbread, filo, rough puff pastry—if it is crumbly, flakey, and melt-in-your-mouth, I can't resist it. Here I share some of my favorite creations, from a fig and wildflower honey crostada (a heavenly, rustic dessert you can tailor depending what fruit is in season) to an ever-so-rich chocolate truffle tart (the little black dress of desserts). Press pastry is my go-to pastry. It is the perfect backdrop to fruit, chocolate, and nut-filled creations. I often make up a double batch and store it in the freezer, ready to pull out when time isn't on my side and I have guests coming for dinner.

01 · When making pastry, handle your ingredients as little as possible and work quickly.

02 · Make sure all of your ingredients are cold before you begin, especially butter and other wet ingredients. During the summer months, I even put my flour and sugar in the refrigerator for 1 hour before using.

03 · Don't be afraid to use a food processor to make your pastry—it can be your best friend.

04 · Work quickly but don't overwork the dough. Blend just until all the ingredients come together.

05 · Once your pastry is mixed, let it rest: roll it into a ball, wrap in plastic wrap, and refrigerate it for a minimum of 1 hour or up to 24 hours. (The gluten in the flour has to have a chance to relax so that the pastry doesn't shrink once it goes in the oven.) Once you have rolled it out, let it rest again for another hour.

06 · When you roll out pastry, lightly flour both your work surface and rolling pin before you begin. Keep moving your pastry on the work surface to make sure it isn't sticking. Be careful not to use too much additional flour—it will make your pastry tough.

07 · When using press pastry, you can line your pan immediately following the mixing, but let it rest in the pan in the refrigerator for at least 1 hour before baking it.

08 · When making crostada, make sure you chill it for at least 1 hour after you have filled it with fruit before baking. It will help the crostada hold its shape.

mini shortbread tarts

makes 4 dozen mini tarts

My friend Linda and I have been making these melt-in-your mouth mini shortbread tarts for years. They are extremely versatile and truly fabulous when filled with lemon curd. At Christmastime I like to fill them with mincemeat or a cranberry compote—there are so many possibilities!

1 cup	unsalted butter	250 mL
1¾ cups	all-purpose flour	425 mL
½ cup	confectioners' (icing) sugar	125 mL

1. In a mixing bowl, using an electric mixer on medium-high speed, cream butter and sugar until light and fluffy. Add flour and mix just until combined.
2. Scrape dough out onto a clean, lightly floured work surface and, using your hands, press into a disk. Wrap disk in plastic wrap and refrigerate for at least 1 hour.
3. Shape dough, 1 tbsp (15 mL) at a time, into even balls. Place a ball in a mini tart pan, using your fingers to press the pastry evenly into the bottom and up the sides. Repeat with remaining balls. Cover and refrigerate for 1 hour or freeze for 15 minutes.
4. Preheat oven to 325°F (160°C).
5. Bake in preheated oven for 15 to 20 minutes. Remove from oven and set aside to cool completely in pan. To release tarts once cool, invert pan and tap gently on the edge of the counter. Store tart shells in an airtight container and refrigerate for up to 3 days or freeze for up to 1 month.
6. When ready to serve, spoon your filling of choice into tarts and garnish.

variations

01 · Fill with lemon curd (page 300) and top with fresh mint.
02 · Fill with chocolate ganache (page 307) and top with fresh raspberries or blackberries, or toasted hazelnuts, pecans, or macadamia nuts.
03 · Fill with homemade preserves (fig, apricot, strawberry, etc.).

lemon soufflé tart with raspberry coulis

makes one 9-inch (23 cm) tart

Don't let the word *soufflé* deter you. This tart is actually really easy to make and worth the little bit of fuss. The trick is making sure you pull it out of the oven right on time: the center should be just set, as it will continue to cook for a few minutes afterward. The result is a light and fluffy tart with a satisfyingly crispy short-crust. Serve it with some fresh berries or raspberry coulis.

•	Press pastry for one 9-inch (23 cm) shell (page 317)	•

filling

4	large free-range eggs, separated	4
6 tbsp + ½ cup	granulated sugar	90 mL + 125 mL
½ cup	freshly squeezed lemon juice, extended to ⅔ cup (150 mL) with water	125 mL
¼ cup	unsalted butter	60 mL
•	Confectioners' (icing) sugar	•
•	Raspberry Coulis (page 298)	•

1. Preheat oven to 375°F (190°C).
2. MAKE FILLING: In a medium bowl, whisk egg yolks and 6 tbsp (90 mL) sugar until pale. Add lemon juice and whisk to combine well. Pour into a medium saucepan over low heat, add butter, and cook, whisking constantly, until butter has melted and mixture has thickened to the consistency of custard. Pour into a shallow pan to cool. Set aside.
3. Line a 9-inch (23 cm) shallow, fluted tart pan with press pastry, pressing dough up the sides to extend ¼ inch (0.5 cm) above rim of the pan. Bake in preheated oven for 15 to 20 minutes, or until top edge of pastry is pale golden. Remove from oven and set aside.
4. Reduce oven temperature to 350°F (180°C).
5. Meanwhile, in a mixing bowl, using an electric mixer on medium-high speed, whisk egg whites and remaining ½ cup (125 mL) sugar until fluffy. Fold in cooled lemon mixture.
6. ASSEMBLE: Spoon filling into baked pastry shell, mounding it a little higher toward the center. Place on baking sheet and bake in reduced-temperature oven for 10 to 15 minutes, or until golden. (Important! Do not open the oven door during first 7 minutes of baking.) Remove pan from oven and place on a wire rack to cool completely. Dust with confectioners' sugar before serving.

tip

For best results, bake and
serve this Lemon Soufflé
Tart the same day and do
not refrigerate. That being
said, I gave one of these tarts
to a friend and she froze
it for a few days, thawed
it out, served it to friends,
and said it was fabulous, so
I will let you be the judge.

lemon blueberry tart

makes one 9-inch (23 cm) tart

No matter how you serve them, lemons and blueberries are a perfect pairing. This tart is light and has a sweet yet refreshing citrus flavor—a great way to finish a luncheon or dinner with friends. Serve with vanilla whipped cream or simply as is. It also pairs well with a nice cup of jasmine or bergamot tea.

	Press pastry for one 9-inch (23 cm) shell (page 317)	

filling

½ cup	freshly squeezed lemon juice	125 mL
2½ tbsp	finely grated lemon zest	37 mL
¼ cup	unsalted butter, melted	60 mL
3	large free-range eggs	3
½ cup	granulated sugar	125 mL

topping

2 cups	fresh blueberries	500 mL
2 tbsp	granulated sugar	30 mL

tip

Do not attempt to make this recipe with frozen berries—they are too soft and give off juice as they thaw, leaving you with a soggy mess. Use fresh berries, preferably local ones in season, for a real treat.

1. Preheat oven to 375°F (190°C).
2. Line a 9-inch (23 cm) shallow, fluted tart pan with press pastry, pressing dough up the sides to extend ⅛ inch (3 mm) above rim of the pan. Bake in preheated oven for 15 to 20 minutes, until top edge of pastry is pale golden. Remove from oven and set aside to cool completely.
3. MAKE FILLING: Meanwhile, in a medium bowl, whisk together lemon juice, lemon zest, and butter. Whisk in eggs and sugar until well combined. Pour into baked shell. Bake in preheated oven for 20 to 25 minutes, or until just barely golden and set. Remove from oven and set aside to cool.
4. SERVE: In a sauté pan over medium-high heat, toss together blueberries and sugar until sugar just barely melts and berries are glossy. Spoon warm berries over top of the tart. (If needed, this can be done a couple hours before serving; just don't refrigerate the finished tart.)

key lime pie

makes one 9-inch (23 cm) pie

Key limes are the smaller, sweeter cousins of everyday limes. Their flavor is very distinct and makes all the difference to this classic pie, so it's worth the extra effort to hunt them down when they're in season. What makes this recipe extra special is the way the slight spice of the gingersnap crust marries perfectly with the sweetly tart pie filling. Top with whipped cream (as we do here) or traditional toasted meringue.

crust

1½ cups	ground gingersnaps or graham crumbs	375 mL
6 tbsp	salted butter, melted	90 mL

filling

4	large free-range eggs	4
1¼ cups	granulated sugar	300 mL
¾ cup	key lime juice	175 mL
1 tsp	finely grated lime zest	5 mL
½ cup	salted butter	125 mL
1¼ cups	heavy or whipping (35%) cream, whipped to soft peaks	300 mL
•	Finely grated key lime zest	•

1. Preheat oven to 325°F (160°C).
2. MAKE CRUST: In a medium bowl, combine gingersnap crumbs and butter. Press mixture into the bottom and up the sides of a 9-inch (23 cm) pie plate. Bake in preheated oven for 10 to 15 minutes, until lightly browned. Remove from oven and set aside to cool completely.
3. MAKE FILLING: Meanwhile, in a medium heatproof glass or metal bowl, whisk together eggs and sugar. Whisk in lime juice and zest. Set over a saucepan of simmering water (make sure water does not touch bottom of bowl) and whisk constantly until mixture starts to thicken like lemon curd, about 10 minutes. Remove from heat and whisk in butter.
4. Pour filling into baked, cooled crust. Cover and refrigerate until chilled, at least 1 hour.
5. FINISH: Remove from fridge. Mound whipped cream on top of the pie and garnish with grated lime zest.

tips

You can make your own graham cracker crumbs by pulsing graham cookies in a food processor until fine. You can also place cookies in a plastic bag and crush them with a rolling pin.

This pie can be made 1 to 2 days in advance, but reserve whipping the cream and topping the pie until just 2 to 3 hours before serving.

If you're a huge key lime fan, it's a good idea to stock up on the limes when they are in season. You can juice them and freeze the spoils for whenever the hankering hits you.

light apple tart barrière poquelin

makes three 7-inch (18 cm) tarts

I've been making a version of this dessert since I was in culinary school in France, and it always instantly transports me back to Paris. It is light, elegant, and literally paper-thin. The lightness, however, doesn't detract anything from the taste—it is bursting with flavor.

tips

You have to keep an eye on this tart as it is baking. If you have any hot spots in your oven, rotate the tart accordingly—you want the sugar to melt as evenly as possible (it will end up having a few brown spots on top, which is fine: you are cooking a thin tart at a very high temperature).

This tart is best eaten the same day it is made, but I have been known to gobble one up for breakfast the next day. For best results, make this as close to serving time as you can. If you need to make it earlier in the day, store it at room temperature (do not refrigerate) and gently reheat before serving.

pastry

2 cups	all-purpose flour	500 mL
¾ cup	cold unsalted butter, cut into ½-inch (1 cm) pieces	175 mL
½ tsp	fine sea salt	2.5 mL

filling

1 to 1½	Granny Smith or Gala apples per tart	1 to 1½
⅓ cup	granulated sugar	75 mL
⅓ cup	cold unsalted butter	75 mL
6 to 7 tbsp	ice-cold water	90 to 105 mL

1. MAKE PASTRY: Preheat oven to 450°F (230°C). Set aside three 7-inch (15 cm) tart pans.
2. In a food processor fitted with the metal blade, combine flour, salt, and butter and pulse until mixture resembles cornmeal. Add just enough water to bring dough together. Scrape dough onto a lightly floured work surface. Using your hands, bring together to form a disk. Wrap in plastic wrap and refrigerate for at least 1 hour.
3. Divide dough into 3 equal portions. Roll each portion out to 1/16–inch (2 mm) thickness. Stretch 1 portion over each tart pan. Roll over the tart pans and let the dough drop into the pan; discard excess dough. Using a fork, prick the pastry all over. Set aside.
4. ASSEMBLE: Core, peel, halve, and thinly slice the apples. Arrange apple slices in slightly overlapping circles, starting in the center and continuing around to completely cover pastry. Sprinkle lightly with sugar. Using a sharp knife, cut butter into paper-thin strips and place on top of the sugar. Bake in preheated oven for 10 to 15 minutes, or until apples are tender and sugar is caramelized. Serve hot with ice cream or semifreddo.

tarte tatin

makes one 10-inch (25 cm) tart

This classic French tart is one of my absolute favorites: not only is it incredibly delicious, but it's also beautiful. I love the moment when you flip it over to reveal all of the caramelized bits of apple. I like to serve it with a traditional crème fraîche, as the tartness of the sauce cuts the sweetness of the sugared apples perfectly, but you can also serve it with good-quality vanilla ice cream and everyone will be very happy.

crust

1½ cups	all-purpose flour	375 mL
2 tbsp	confectioners' (icing) sugar	30 mL
½ cup	cold unsalted butter, cut into ½-inch (1 cm) cubes	125 mL
2½ tbsp	ice-cold water	37 mL
1	large free-range egg	1

filling

¾ cup	granulated sugar	175 mL
2 tbsp	salted butter	30 mL
7 to 8	medium Granny Smith apples, peeled, cored, halved	6 to 7

1. MAKE CRUST: In a food processor fitted with the metal blade, add flour, sugar, and salt and pulse until blended. Add butter and pulse about 12 to 14 times, until butter pieces are the size of peas.
2. In a small bowl, whisk together water and egg. With food processor running, add all at once to dry ingredients. Stop the processor as soon as the dough starts to come together into a ball.
3. Turn dough out onto a lightly floured work surface. Gather dough into a ball and gently press into a disk. Wrap in parchment paper or plastic wrap and refrigerate until chilled, at least 1 hour.
4. MAKE FILLING: Meanwhile, in a 10-inch (25 cm) cast-iron pan or other ovenproof skillet or metal pan, over medium heat, combine sugar and butter and cook until the sugar dissolves and starts to caramelize. Swirl the pan for even coloring. Form an outer circle of apple halves by carefully placing them, round-side down, into the caramel. Then place enough additional apple halves to form an inner circle and fill the entire pan. Simmer slowly on top of the stove until the apples

continued . . .

are entirely caramelized and soft but not falling apart, 30 to 40 minutes. Turn the apples over partway through the cooking to caramelize on all sides, but make sure you finish with the rounded side of the apple halves facing down. Remove from heat.

5. Preheat oven to 350°F (180°C).

6. Remove chilled dough from refrigerator. On a lightly floured work surface, roll out the dough into a circle about ¼ inch (0.5 cm) thick and 1 inch (2.5 cm) wider in diameter than your skillet. Roll loosely around rolling pin and unroll over the apples. Fold the overhanging pastry in toward the center so it totally covers the apples and fits the skillet. Bake in preheated oven for 30 to 40 minutes, or until caramel is bubbling around the edges and pastry is golden. Remove from oven and cool in pan for 15 minutes or so.

7. Place a large platter face down over the pan. Holding both firmly, carefully invert the pan to release the tart onto the platter.

tip

Take your time releasing the tart from the pan. After inverting the pan onto the plate, be sure that the tart has time to "settle" before you lift the pan off or you may end up pulling it apart.

See my YouTube video for how to make Tarte Tatin.

apple almond custard tart

makes one 9-inch (23 cm) tart

This creamy, caramelly, rustic tart looks simple but is filled with layers of texture and flavor. I love to serve this in fall when apples are in season and the warm caramel can chase away the chill in the air. It's cosy comfort food.

•	Press pastry for one 9-inch (23 cm) shell (page 317)	•

apples

¾ cup	unsalted butter	175 mL
¾ cup	granulated sugar	175 mL
5	baking apples, peeled, cored, and cut into sixths	5

custard

¼ cup	heavy or whipping (35%) cream	60 mL
1	large free-range egg	1
½ tsp	pure vanilla extract	2.5 mL
¼ cup	ground almonds	60 mL
¼ cup	Caramel Sauce (page 305)	60 mL
Generous pinch	ground cinnamon	Generous pinch

tip

This tart is best served at room temperature, so if you make it the day before you need it, refrigerate it overnight but make sure you pull it out of the fridge at least 1 hour beforehand to bring it to room temperature before serving.

1. Preheat oven to 375°F (190°C).
2. Line a 9-inch (23 cm) shallow, fluted tart pan with press pastry, pressing dough up the sides to extend ¼ inch (0.5 cm) above rim of the pan. Bake in preheated oven for 15 to 20 minutes, or until top edge of pastry is slightly pale golden. Remove from oven and set aside.
3. Reduce oven temperature to 350°F (180°C).
4. PREPARE APPLES: Meanwhile, in a large saucepan over low heat, melt butter. Add sugar and stir until dissolved. Add apple slices and toss to coat. Cook for about 5 minutes, just until the apples soften slightly. Remove pan from heat and set aside.
5. MAKE CUSTARD: In a mixing bowl, using an electric mixer on medium-high speed, mix cream, egg, and vanilla until well combined. Add almonds, caramel, and cinnamon and mix until well combined. Set aside.
6. Fill baked pastry shell with prepared apple slices. Pour custard over apples. Place filled tart pan on baking sheet. Bake in reduced-temperature oven for 20 to 30 minutes, or until set and slightly golden. Remove pan from oven and place on wire rack to cool completely before serving. Serve with Crème Anglaise (page 303), Vanilla Ice Cream (page 230), Salted Caramel Ice Cream (page 232), or Vanilla Semifreddo (page 220).

crème brûlée tart with blackberries

makes one 9-inch (23 cm) tart

This isn't the crème brûlée with the crispy top that you can crack through with your spoon. Instead it's a caramelized sugar topping over a rich and creamy fruit-filled custard. Delicious—and worth the effort that goes into making it.

6	large free-range egg yolks	6
6 tbsp	granulated sugar	90 mL
2 cups	heavy or whipping (35%) cream	500 mL
1 cup	sour cream	250 mL
1 tsp	pure vanilla extract	5 mL
¼ cup	unsalted butter	60 mL
•	Press pastry for one 9-inch (23 cm) shell (page 317)	•
¼ cup	unsalted butter	60 mL
2 oz	70% bittersweet (dark) chocolate	60 g
1 cup	fresh blackberries	250 mL
•	Golden brown sugar	•

1. In a medium heatproof glass or metal bowl, whisk together egg yolks and sugar. Whisk in cream, sour cream, vanilla, and butter. Set bowl over a saucepan of simmering water (make sure water does not touch bottom of bowl) and stir constantly until mixture thickens to the consistency of lemon curd, about 10 minutes. Remove pan from the heat and set aside to cool slightly, then cover and refrigerate until completely chilled, at least 3 hours or preferably overnight.
2. Preheat oven to 350°F (180°C).
3. Line a 9-inch (23 cm) shallow, fluted tart pan with press pastry, pressing dough up the sides to extend ⅛ inch (3 mm) above rim of the pan. Bake in preheated oven for 15 to 20 minutes, until top edge of pastry is pale golden but pastry is cooked through on the bottom. Remove pan from oven and set aside to cool completely.
4. Meanwhile, in a small heavy-bottomed saucepan over low heat, melt butter and chocolate, stirring to combine. Remove from the heat and pour into baked, cooled pastry shell. Let set for 15 minutes.
5. Turn on oven broiler.
6. Arrange berries in a single layer on top of the chocolate in the pastry shell. Spoon the chilled filling over top, completely covering the berries. Using a fine-mesh sieve, sprinkle a fine layer of brown sugar over the surface of the filling. Place tart on top rack under broiler just until sugar melts and starts to bubble, 2 to 3 minutes. Remove from oven, let cool slightly, then refrigerate until ready to serve.

tip

I've used blackberries here because I love them—they offer robust flavor without all the sweetness of berries such as strawberries—but you can use whichever berry is fresh and in season and it will still work really well.

papaya passion fruit tart

makes one 9-inch (23 cm) tart

The tropical flavors of papaya and passion fruit make this tart taste like a burst of
sunshine no matter what time of year you're enjoying it. And it's so pretty that it's often
my go-to for a special occasion instead of cake. To get the papaya perfectly uniform for
the topping, use a potato peeler to slice off even pieces and then trim the overhanging
excess with a sharp paring knife. The macadamia nuts are optional but add to the
tropical taste if you do choose to use them.

•	Press pastry for one 9-inch (23 cm) shell (page 317)	•
	almond filling	
½ cup	granulated sugar	125 mL
½ cup	slivered almonds	125 mL
•	Finely grated zest and juice of 1½ oranges	•
6 tbsp	unsalted butter, melted	90 mL
2	large free-range eggs	2

cream cheese filling

½ cup	passion fruit juice	125 mL
¼ cup	unsalted butter, softened	60 mL
¼ cup	confectioners' (icing) sugar	60 mL
6 oz	cream cheese, softened	175 g
1 tsp	orange zest	5 mL
1	ripe papaya	1
¼ cup	apricot preserves, to glaze	60 mL
16	macadamia nuts, halved, dusted with confectioners' sugar	16
·	Sprig of fresh mint	·

continued . . .

1. Preheat oven to 350°F (180°C).
2. Line a 9-inch (23 cm) shallow, fluted tart pan with press pastry, pressing dough up the sides to extend ⅛ inch (3 mm) above rim of the pan. Bake in preheated oven for 15 to 20 minutes, or until top edge of pastry is pale golden. Remove from oven and set aside.
3. MAKE ALMOND FILLING: In a food processor fitted with the metal blade, add sugar and almonds and pulse until very fine and sand-like. Transfer to a medium bowl. Add orange juice and zest, melted butter, and eggs and whisk together to combine. Pour into baked pastry shell. Bake in preheated oven for 20 to 25 minutes, or until just set and lightly golden. Remove from oven and set aside to cool.
4. MAKE CREAM CHEESE FILLING: Meanwhile, in a small saucepan over medium heat, bring passion fruit juice to a boil. Simmer until reduced to about 1 tbsp (15 mL). Remove pan from heat and set aside to cool to room temperature.
5. In a small bowl, using a wooden spoon, stir together butter, confectioners' sugar, and cream cheese until well combined. Add cooled passion fruit reduction and orange zest. Stir to combine. Gently spread over top of baked and cooled almond filling. Set aside.
6. Peel papaya, cut in half lengthwise, and scoop out seeds and membrane. Cut papaya in long, thin, even slices starting at the top/stem end. Lay overlapping slices to cover the top of the cream cheese filling to create a spiral effect, with narrow ends pointing toward the center.
7. ASSEMBLE: In a small saucepan over low heat, melt the apricot preserves, adding a little water to thin if necessary. Brush lightly over papaya slices. Garnish with macadamia nuts placed evenly around outside edge of tart. Arrange sprig of mint in center of tart. Refrigerate until ready to serve.

tip
....
This tart can be prepared
in two parts: the pastry
and filling one day (just
cover and refrigerate), and
the cream cheese, papaya,
and glaze the next.

white-chocolate satin tart
with raspberries

makes one 9-inch (23 cm) tart

This dessert is perfect for special gatherings or formal dinners. It looks spectacular and tastes even better. Use only the freshest berries when they are in season—it really will make all the difference.

	Press pastry for one 9-inch (23 cm) shell (page 317)	
¼ cup	unsalted butter	60 mL
2 oz	70% bittersweet (dark) chocolate, roughly chopped	60 g
1 cup	fresh raspberries	250 mL
	filling	
6 oz	white chocolate, roughly chopped	175 g
¾ cup	unsalted butter, softened	175 mL
1 cup	confectioners' (icing) sugar	250 mL
3	large cold free-range eggs	3
2 tbsp	Chocolate Ganache (page 307)	30 mL

1. Preheat oven to 375°F (190°C).
2. Line a 9-inch (23 cm) shallow, fluted tart pan with press pastry, pressing dough up the sides to extend ¼ inch (0.5 cm) above rim of the pan. Bake in preheated oven for 15 to 20 minutes, or until top edge of pastry is pale golden. Remove from oven and set aside to cool to room temperature.
3. In a small saucepan over low heat, melt butter and dark chocolate, stirring constantly until smooth. Pour into cooled pastry shell. Set aside for about 15 minutes to set. Once chocolate is set, arrange raspberries evenly over chocolate. Set aside.
4. MAKE FILLING: Meanwhile, in a small metal or glass bowl set over a saucepan of simmering water (make sure water does not touch bottom of bowl), melt white chocolate, stirring constantly. Remove from heat and set aside.
5. In a separate bowl, whisk eggs well and set aside.
6. In a large mixing bowl, using an electric mixer on medium-high speed, cream butter and sugar until light and fluffy. Slowly add melted chocolate and mix until well combined. Add prepared eggs and mix until thick and satiny.

7. Spoon filling into baked pastry shell, covering raspberries and mounding a little higher toward the center.

8. DECORATE: In a small saucepan over low heat, melt ganache, stirring constantly until smooth. Spoon into a pastry bag with a ⅛-inch (3 mm) plain tip or a resealable bag with the tip snipped off. Starting at the center of the tart, pipe concentric circles, spacing them about ½ inch (1 cm) apart. To create a spiderweb effect, lightly place the point of a knife at the center of the tart and draw it through the chocolate circles to the edge of the tart. Give the tart a quarter turn and repeat. Once the top is divided equally by 4 lines, draw the knife point through each quarter 4 times.

variation

Substitute the raspberries with
an equal amount of fresh blackberries
when they come into season
at the end of the summer.

toasted macadamia coconut tart

makes one 9-inch (23 cm) tart

The combination of coconut and macadamia nuts always reminds me of the South Pacific, and this delicious, rich tart delivers a taste of the tropics with every bite. Watch the oven closely when you are toasting the nuts, as things can go from golden brown to overdone in the blink of an eye. I love serving this with heavy cream whipped to soft peaks and then crème fraîche folded in. The crème fraîche cuts the sweetness of the tart and the heavy cream offers a soft lightness to the topping.

tip

If you're looking for extra flavor, you could add 1 tsp (5 mL) of vanilla or Cointreau to the cream before whipping in step 7.

filling

3 oz	unsalted butter	90 g
⅝ cup	packed golden brown sugar	155 mL
3 tbsp	liquid honey	45 mL
3 tbsp	heavy or whipping (35%) cream	45 mL
3	large free-range egg yolks	3
1 tsp	pure vanilla extract	5 mL
1¼ cups	macadamia nuts, toasted	300 mL
½ cup	ribbon coconut, toasted	125 mL
•	Press pastry for one 9-inch (23 cm) shell (page 317)	•

topping

1 cup	heavy or whipping (35%) cream	250 mL
⅓ cup	crème fraîche or Greek yogurt	75 mL

1. Preheat oven to 375°F (190°C).
2. MAKE FILLING: In a medium heavy-bottomed saucepan over low heat, melt butter with brown sugar and honey. Remove from heat and set aside to cool slightly.
3. In a medium bowl, whisk together cream, egg yolks, and vanilla. Slowly whisk in brown sugar mixture. Stir in nuts and coconut and combine well.
4. Line a 9-inch (23 cm) shallow, fluted tart pan with press pastry, pressing dough up the sides to extend ¼ inch (0.5 cm) above rim of the pan. Bake in preheated oven for 15 to 20 minutes, or until top edge of pastry is slightly pale golden. Remove from oven.
5. Reduce oven temperature to 350°F (180°C).
6. Pour filling into baked pastry shell. Place filled tart pan on a baking sheet. Bake in reduced-temperature oven for 20 to 25 minutes, or until top edge of pastry is pale golden and filling is set. Remove from oven and place on a wire rack to cool completely before serving.
7. MAKE TOPPING: In a mixing bowl, using an electric mixer on medium-high speed, whip cream until soft peaks form. Fold in crème fraîche. Spoon over filling.

caramel nut crunch tart with chocolate truffle pastry

makes one 9-inch (23 cm) tart

A nut lover's dream, this tart is easy to make and very versatile. It calls for 4 cups (1 L) of nuts, and you can mix and match whatever combination of nuts you have on hand. Before serving, drizzle with ganache for an added special touch.

	Chocolate truffle press pastry for one 9-inch (23 cm) shell (page 317)	
1½ cups	granulated sugar	375 mL
1 cup	water	250 mL
1 cup	heavy or whipping (35%) cream	250 mL
¾ cup	unsalted butter	175 mL
⅓ cup	liquid honey	75 mL
2 cups	Thompson raisins	500 mL
4 cups	nuts (whole almonds, cashews, halved macadamia nuts), toasted	1 L
	Chocolate Ganache (page 307)	

1. Preheat oven to 375°F (190°C).
2. In a medium heavy-bottomed saucepan over medium heat, bring sugar and water to a boil. Reduce heat and simmer until mixture starts to turn golden. For more even caramelizing, swirl the mixture in the pan several times—*do not stir with a spoon at this stage*. Cook until a deep amber color, but watch carefully as it can burn quickly. Remove from heat and very slowly pour in cream (it will bubble up furiously and then subside). Return saucepan to stove over low heat and stir to combine. Stir in butter and honey, and continue cooking until thickened to the consistency of honey. Stir in nuts and raisins. Remove from heat and set aside to cool to room temperature.
3. Line 9-inch (23 cm) shallow, fluted tart pan with chocolate truffle press pastry, gently pressing dough up the sides to extend ¼ inch (0.5 cm) above rim of the pan. Bake in preheated oven for about 20 minutes, or until pastry looks dry and set. Remove from oven.
4. Reduce oven temperature to 350°F (180°C).
5. Spoon filling into baked pastry shell to ¼ inch (0.5 cm) below the rim of shell. Place filled tart pan on baking sheet. Bake in reduced-temperature oven for 30 minutes, or until crust is lightly brown and filling is set. Remove pan from oven and place on a wire rack to cool completely before serving.

fig and hazelnut crostata

makes one 9-inch (23 cm) crostata

This is the perfect dessert for those who love to bake but don't want to get fussy with the decorating. All you need to do is roll the easy-to-make dough out to the appropriate size, pile the filling in the center, and then fold the pastry in around itself. It's rustic-looking and beautiful. As with most of the fruit-based recipes in this book, if you can't get fresh figs you can always substitute with either dried figs or other fresh fruit, as desired. Apricot and cherry is a favorite combination around our house.

filling

2 lbs	fresh figs, smaller halved and larger quartered	1 kg
1 cup	halved hazelnuts, lightly toasted	250 mL
½ cup	liquid honey	125 mL
¼ cup	packed golden brown sugar	60 mL
2 tbsp	cornstarch	30 mL
½ tsp	fine sea salt	2.5 mL
1 tbsp	grated orange zest	15 mL
1 tbsp	brandy	15 mL
½ recipe	Sweet Tart Dough (page 319)	½ recipe
·	Heavy or whipping (35%) cream	·
·	Coarse sugar	·

1. Preheat oven to 350°F (180°C). Line a baking sheet with parchment paper.
2. In a large bowl, gently toss figs and hazelnuts in honey.
3. In a separate bowl, stir together brown sugar, cornstarch, salt, and orange zest. Gently fold into fig mixture. Sprinkle brandy over top.
4. On a lightly floured work surface, roll dough into a circle ¼ inch (0.5 cm) thick and 11 inches (28 cm) in diameter. Drape over a rolling pin and transfer to prepared baking sheet.
5. Spoon filling in the center of the pastry, leaving a 2-inch (5 cm) border. Gently fold overhanging edges of the pastry up around the filling, letting it drape inward (it is meant to look somewhat rustic). Brush the edges with cream and sprinkle heavily with coarse sugar. Bake in preheated oven for 20 to 25 minutes, or until filling is bubbling and pastry is golden. Remove from oven and cool for a few minutes before serving.

bittersweet chocolate tart

makes one 9-inch (23 cm) tart

This tart is the ultimate chocolate lover's dream! Deep, satiny-smooth bittersweet chocolate atop a crisp crust . . . simply perfection. A good choice would be Manjari chocolate, which comes from the best cocoa beans in the Madagascar region and has a slightly smoky, fruity flavor. Valrhona is a good supplier if you can get it in your area, but if not then any good-quality chocolate will do.

•	Press pastry for one 9-inch (23 cm) shell (page 317)	•

	filling	
1¼ cups	heavy or whipping (35%) cream	300 mL
⅛ tsp	fine sea salt	0.5 mL
¼ cup	unsalted butter, softened	60 mL
7 oz	70% bittersweet (dark) Manjari chocolate, broken into small pieces	210 g
2 tbsp	salted butter	30 mL

•	Caramel Chunks (page 76) or fresh berries	•
•	Fresh mint leaves	•
•	Confectioners' (icing) sugar	•

1. Preheat oven to 350°F (180°C).
2. Line a 9-inch (23 cm) shallow, fluted tart pan with press pastry, pressing dough up the sides to extend ¼ inch (0.5 cm) above rim of the pan. Bake in preheated oven for about 15 minutes, or until firm. Remove pan from oven and place on a wire rack to cool completely.
3. MAKE FILLING: In a heavy-bottomed saucepan over medium heat, bring cream and salt to a boil. Remove from heat as soon as the mixture boils. Add butter and chocolate and stir until chocolate is melted and mixture is smooth. Remove pan from heat and set aside for 2 minutes. Add butter and stir until the mixture is shiny.
4. ASSEMBLE: Pour filling into baked, cooled pastry shell. Set aside at room temperature for 2 hours to allow filling to set. If desired, decorate with fresh berries or a mound of Caramel Chunks (see page 76).

variation

This recipe can be adapted to satisfy a variety of tastes: mix it up with different berries or even hazelnuts, macadamia nuts, or caramelized pecans.

Bittersweet Chocolate Tart (page 115) and *Caramel Nut Crunch Tart with Chocolate Truffle Pastry* (page 110)

verona's arborio tart

makes one 9-inch (23 cm) tart

At first blush the plump fruits, crunchy pine nuts, and savoury sweet rice in this tart may seem a little surprising, but once you've made it, I promise you'll keep coming back to this recipe whenever you're looking for an easy, crowd-pleasing dessert. Of course, you don't need to wait for dinner. It's just as nice with a cup of mid-afternoon tea as it is with a short espresso for breakfast.

Press pastry for one 9-inch (23 cm) shell (page 317)

2½ cups	whole milk, divided	625 mL
⅓ cup	arborio rice	75 mL
⅓ cup	heavy or whipping (35%) cream	75 mL
¼ cup	granulated sugar	60 mL
3 tbsp	golden raisins, soaked in warm water for 15 minutes and drained	45 mL
3 tbsp	chopped pitted dates	45 mL
3 tbsp	pine nuts, toasted	45 mL
1½ tsp	finely grated orange zest	7 mL
⅓ tsp	ground cinnamon	2.6 mL
½ tsp	pure vanilla extract	2.5 mL
3	large free-range egg yolks	3

tips

Be sure to use arborio rice (the same used in risotto), as it absorbs the liquids and becomes gorgeously creamy.

I think this tart is best eaten the day it is made, but it will keep overnight in the refrigerator. Just be sure to pull it out of the fridge 1 hour or so before needed so you can bring it to room temperature before serving it.

For a simpler version, omit the dried fruit and nuts and add ½ tsp (2.5 mL) of freshly grated lemon zest.

1. Preheat oven to 375°F (190°C).
2. Line a 9-inch (23 cm) shallow, fluted tart pan with press pastry, pressing dough up the sides to extend ¼ inch (0.5 cm) above rim of the pan. Bake in preheated oven for 15 to 20 minutes, or until top edge of pastry is pale golden. Remove pan from oven and set aside.
3. Reduce oven temperature to 350°F (180°C).
4. In a heavy-bottomed saucepan over medium heat, bring 2 cups (500 mL) milk and rice to a boil. Reduce heat and simmer for 15 minutes. Stir in remaining ½ cup (125 mL) milk, cream, sugar, raisins, dates, pine nuts, orange zest, cinnamon, and vanilla and bring back to a simmer. Remove from heat and, one at a time and mixing after each addition, stir in egg yolks until well combined.
5. Pour filling into baked pastry shell and spread evenly. Place filled tart pan on a baking sheet and bake in reduced-temperature oven for 20 to 30 minutes, or until set and light golden. Remove pan from oven and place on wire rack to cool completely before serving.

cakes

for best results

When most people think of cake, they imagine towering, multilayered sponge with swirls of frosting. My cakes have been developed over years of experimenting, with input from clients and the desire to break from tradition. Some are grand enough for special occasions, but many are simply irresistible any day of the week. Get ready to be wowed by intense and sticky single-layer chocolate cakes, meringue nut cakes layered with cream and fruit purée, and a dense almond paste cake that will make you swoon (it's one of my favourite go-to cakes served with cream and local berries). Follow the tips here for great results.

01 · Carefully follow the instructions for greasing, flouring, and lining cake pans. It will make turning out the cakes so much easier and give you much cleaner results for finishing.

02 · When beating egg whites to fold into a cake batter, be careful not to overmix them. If they become dry and start separating, it will be very hard to incorporate them and you will end up overworking your batter.

03 · When testing for doneness, some of the recipes in this chapter call for a moist center. The best way to check is by inserting a wooden skewer into the center of the cake. Once the skewer is removed, there should be some moist crumbs attached, but it should not be wet.

04 · Sponge cakes are cooked when the top has an even, golden color and the sides of the cake have pulled away from the pan slightly.

05 · Once removed from the oven, do not leave baked cakes in the pans for too long. It is easier to unmold them when they are still warm.

06 · When you make a meringue cake (for example, a pavlova or dacquoise), once it is finished baking, leave it in the oven for at least 1 hour but ideally 4 hours or overnight so it will cool slowly. This will prevent it from cracking.

07 · Cool cake completely before slicing.

08 · Use a hot, wet chef's knife to slice and serve dense, moist cakes. Use a serrated knife to neatly cut through meringue cakes.

tuscan sabayon cake

makes one 9-inch (23 cm) cake

This cake is a bit of work, but worth every bit of effort you put in. With its light Tuscan sponge layers separated by rich sabayon cream and its over-the-top white-chocolate curls, this has always been the most popular choice around our house for special events such as milestone birthdays, anniversaries, and even weddings. Once you've made it, be prepared for the onslaught of requests to make it again and again.

sponge

2½ cups	all-purpose flour	625 mL
5 tsp	baking powder	25 mL
Pinch	fine sea salt	Pinch
10	large free-range eggs, separated	10
2½ cups	granulated sugar	625 mL
½ cup + 2 tbsp	boiling water	125 mL + 30 mL
2 tsp	pure vanilla extract	10 mL

sabayon

11	large free-range egg yolks	11
½ cup	granulated sugar	125 mL
Pinch	fine sea salt	Pinch
¾ cup	champagne	175 mL
1 cup	heavy or whipping (35%) cream	250 mL
1½ lbs	block white chocolate	750 g

tip

See my YouTube video on how to make chocolate curls.

1. Preheat oven to 350°F (180°C). Line 3 baking sheets with parchment paper. Line the bottom of a 9-inch (23 cm) springform pan with parchment paper.

2. MAKE SPONGE: In a medium bowl, sift together flour, baking powder, and salt. Set aside.

3. In a medium mixing bowl, using an electric mixer on medium-high speed, beat yolks and sugar until pale and frothy. Mix in water and vanilla. Fold in the dry ingredients.

4. In another medium mixing bowl, beat egg whites to soft peaks. Fold into yolk mixture. Divide into 3 equal portions and pour onto prepared baking sheets, using a spatula to spread mixture evenly to the edges of the sheets. Bake in preheated oven for 15 minutes. Remove pans from oven and set aside to cool. Cut the sponge into six 9-inch (23 cm) rounds (use the base of a 9-inch/23 cm cake pan as a guide). Set aside.

continued...

5. MAKE SABAYON: In another mixing bowl, using an electric mixer on medium-high speed, whip cream to soft peaks. Set aside.

6. Fill a large bowl with ice and set aside.

7. In another large heatproof bowl, whisk together yolks, sugar, salt, and champagne. Place over a saucepan of simmering water (do not let water touch bottom of bowl) and whisk mixture constantly until thick and foamy. Remove pan from the heat and place over ice in bowl, continuing to whisk until cool. Fold in whipped cream. Set aside.

8. ASSEMBLE: Place one layer of sponge on bottom of prepared springform pan. Cover with 1 cup (250 mL) sabayon mixture. Repeat with the remaining layers, reserving some sabayon for icing sides, ending with a layer of sabayon on top. Release cake from springform pan and place on a serving platter. Cover sides of sponge with remaining sabayon.

9. Pull the edge of a large chef's knife across the block of chocolate to create decorative shavings for sides of cake. Rub the edge of the chocolate with the heel of your hand to soften it slightly, then, using a vegetable peeler, peel curls of chocolate off the block for decorating the top of the cake. Cover the sides of the cake with the shavings and the top with the curls (they will stick to the sabayon). Refrigerate cake until ready to serve.

tip

This cake can be assembled the day before and kept refrigerated until serving or frozen for up to 1 week in advance.

lemon almond meringue gâteau

makes one 9-inch (23 cm) cake

This cake is for all those people who like their desserts light and lemony. I love the layers of feather-light meringue, dense almond cake, tart lemon curd, and fresh whipped cream so much that this has always been my go-to base for wedding cakes (it's also my son Douglas's favorite birthday cake). It may sound complicated, but if you have all of the pieces ready to go, it comes together fairly easily.

sponge cake

½ cup	all-purpose flour	125 mL
⅛ tsp	fine sea salt	0.5 mL
3	large free-range eggs	3
⅓ cup + 1 tbsp	granulated sugar	175 mL + 15 mL
½ tsp	pure vanilla extract	2.5 mL

meringues

4	large free-range egg whites	4
¼ tsp	fine sea salt	1 mL
½ cup + 2 tbsp	granulated sugar	125 mL + 30 mL
¼ tsp	pure vanilla extract	1 mL
1 cup	ground almonds	250 mL

lemon syrup

•	Juice of 2 lemons	•
½ cup	granulated sugar	125 mL

1 cup	Lemon Curd (page 300)	250 mL
3 cups	heavy or whipping (35%) cream, whipped	750 mL
1 cup	flaked almonds, toasted	250 mL
•	Confectioners' (icing) sugar	•

1. Preheat oven to 325°F (160°C). Butter and flour a 9-inch (23 cm) springform pan.
2. MAKE SPONGE: Sift flour and measure into a medium bowl. Add salt. Set aside.
3. In a large nonreactive bowl set over a saucepan of simmering water (make sure water does not touch bottom of bowl), whisk together eggs and sugar and warm slightly. Remove from heat. Add vanilla, and beat until the mixture holds a ribbon when you lift the beater (the mixture should leave a trail that lasts for a few seconds). Using a whisk, fold in dry ingredients in 4 portions quickly but gently.

continued . . .

Give the whisk a shake each time you bring it up through the batter to break up any lumps of flour. Pour into prepared springform pan. Bake in preheated oven for 30 to 35 minutes, or until the top springs back when lightly pressed. Remove pan from oven and place on a wire rack to cool.

4. Reduce oven temperature to 300°F (150°C). Line 2 baking sheets with parchment paper. Set an 8½-inch (21 cm) dinner plate in the center of the parchment paper and draw around the outside with a pencil to create a guide for piping. Turn the paper over. Repeat on other parchment paper.

5. MAKE MERINGUES: In a mixing bowl, using an electric mixer on medium-high speed, beat egg whites with salt until stiff peaks form. Add sugar and vanilla and beat at least 2 minutes more, or until glossy. Gently fold in almonds. Gently spoon into pastry bag with a #4 or ½-inch (1 cm) plain tip. Starting in the center of the circle on the prepared baking sheet, pipe the meringue in a spiral pattern out to the penciled border. Bake in preheated oven for 1 hour, or until the meringue is firm and dry and faintly colored (it will expand slightly as it bakes). Remove from oven and cool on pan. Set aside.

6. MAKE LEMON SYRUP: In a small saucepan over medium heat, combine lemon juice and sugar and cook, whisking constantly, until sugar dissolves. Remove from heat and set aside to cool.

7. ASSEMBLE: Cut sponge cake crosswise into 2 portions. Lay cut-side up and brush lemon syrup evenly over both sponges. On a cardboard cake board or a flat plate, assemble layers: 1 portion of sponge cake, cut-side up; ⅓ cup (75 mL) lemon curd; ¾ cup (175 mL) whipped cream; 1 meringue; ⅓ cup (75 mL) lemon curd; ¾ cup (175 mL) whipped cream; 1 portion of sponge cake, cut-side up; ⅓ cup (75 mL) lemon curd; ¾ cup (175 mL) whipped cream; 1 meringue. Cover the top and sides with ¾ cup (175 mL) whipped cream. Press almonds over the top and sides. Dust with confectioners' sugar.

tip

Don't be intimidated by the steps in this recipe. You can make the lemon curd, syrup, sponge, and meringue a few days in advance. Keep the curd in an airtight container in the refrigerator, the sponge in an airtight container in the freezer, and the meringue in an airtight container at room temperature. Then just whip the cream and assemble the cake on the day you want to serve it.

apricot dacquoise with passion fruit coulis

This elegant dessert marries layers of meringue with whipped cream and fresh apricots and passion fruit. It's light, delicious, and sure to impress.

dacquoise

⅓ cup	whole blanched almonds	75 mL
4	large free-range egg whites	4
1 cup	granulated sugar	250 mL

filling

1 cup	chopped dried apricots	250 mL
½ cup	water	125 mL
½ cup	granulated sugar	125 mL
1½ cups	heavy or whipping (35%) cream	375 mL

coulis

½ cup	fresh passion fruit purée or frozen passion fruit purée, thawed	125 mL
⅓ cup	granulated sugar	75 mL
·	Confectioners' (icing) sugar	·
·	10 fresh mint leaves	·

1. Preheat oven to 250°F (120°C). Line a 13- by 9-inch (33 by 23 cm) baking sheet with parchment paper.
2. MAKE DACQUOISE: Soak almonds in a small bowl of boiling water for 10 minutes. Drain and pat dry with paper towel. In a food processor fitted with the metal blade, finely grind almonds. Set aside.
3. In a medium bowl, using an electric mixer on medium-high speed, whisk egg whites until stiff but not dry. Gradually add half of the sugar and whisk until stiff and shiny, 3 to 4 minutes. Fold in remaining sugar and ground almonds until just combined (be careful not to overmix).
4. On prepared baking sheet, divide batter into 2 oblong shapes, each measuring about 13 by 3½ inches (33 by 8.5 cm). Bake in preheated oven for 1 hour, or until dry and firm. Turn oven off and let sit in oven for 1 hour. Remove from oven and set baking sheet aside.

continued . . .

5. MAKE FILLING: Meanwhile, in a small saucepan over low heat, combine apricots, water, and sugar and cook until apricots are tender. Transfer to a food processor fitted with the metal blade and purée until smooth (the mixture should be thick but spreadable, like preserves or jam). Set aside to cool, reserving 3 tbsp (45 mL) in a separate bowl.

6. MAKE COULIS: In a small saucepan over medium-high heat, combine passion fruit purée and sugar and bring to a boil. Reduce heat and simmer until purée has reduced and slightly thickened. Remove from heat. Cool and refrigerate to chill.

7. In a mixing bowl, using an electric mixer on medium-high speed, whip cream until stiff but not dry peaks form.

8. ASSEMBLE: Spread half of the apricot filling over 1 dacquoise layer. Top with whipped cream, reserving ½ cup (125 mL) for decorating, and spread evenly. Using a fork, gently spread remaining apricot filling over top. Dust top of second dacquoise with confectioners' sugar and place on top of filling.

9. Spoon the reserved ½ cup (125 mL) whipped cream into a pastry bag fitted with a star tip (for piping rosettes). Pipe 10 equally spaced rosettes across the top of the dacquoise. Decorate with mint leaves. Refrigerate until ready to serve.

10. FINISH: Use a serrated knife to cut slices. Place a slice on a serving plate and spoon several small pools of coulis around it.

tip

There are several tricks to making meringue: ensure that all of your equipment—bowls, spatulas, measuring spoons—are completely clean, that your eggs are at room temperature before you begin, and that you beat your egg whites until they are stiff but not dry before you add the sugar. The sugar acts as a stabilizer, so you shouldn't experience any trouble after that—just be gentle when you fold in any additions.

bavarian apple torte

makes one 9-inch (23 cm) torte

This is my sister Marianne's absolute favorite cake. It was also the most popular with the staff in my fine foods shop in Vancouver, who were very, very happy the odd time one hadn't sold by the end of the day. And what's not to love? A traditional baked cheesecake atop a shortbread crust covered with cinnamony apples—delicious!

crust

½ cup	unsalted butter, softened	125 mL
⅓ cup	granulated sugar	75 mL
1 cup	all-purpose flour	250 mL

filling

3 oz	cream cheese, softened	90 g
1 cup + 2 tbsp	granulated sugar	250 mL + 30 mL
4	large free-range eggs, at room temperature	4
1 tsp	pure vanilla extract	5 mL
3	Granny Smith apples, peeled, cored, and cut into ¼-inch (0.5 cm) slices	3
1 tsp	ground cinnamon	5 mL

1. **MAKE CRUST:** In a mixing bowl, on medium-high speed, cream together butter and sugar. Add flour and mix just until it comes together to form a moist (but not sticky) dough.
2. Turn dough out onto a lightly floured work surface and, using your hands, press into a flat disk. Roll out to an 11-inch (28 cm) circle. Line a 9-inch (23 cm) springform pan with the pastry, pressing dough to extend 2 inches (5 cm) up the sides of the pan. Refrigerate for at least 1 hour.
3. Remove crust from fridge. Preheat oven to 350°F (180°C).
4. **MAKE FILLING:** In a mixing bowl, on medium-high speed, beat cream cheese until light and fluffy. Gradually beat in 1 cup (250 mL) sugar until well combined. One at a time, mixing well between each addition, add eggs. Add vanilla and mix well. Set aside.
5. **ASSEMBLE:** In a medium bowl, combine remaining 2 tbsp (30 mL) sugar and cinnamon. Add apple slices and toss to coat well.
6. Pour the cream cheese mixture into the pastry-lined pan. Starting from the outside edge, gently arrange the apple slices, overlapping, in a circle, continuing with increasingly smaller circles until the entire surface is covered.
7. Bake in preheated oven for 45 to 55 minutes, until light golden and the filling has set. Remove from oven and set aside to cool to room temperature. Refrigerate for at least 1 hour before serving.

upside-down pear gingerbread cake

This is a classic cold-weather dessert that contains all the best flavors of fall: juicy pears, spicy gingerbread, and rich caramel. Don't be in a rush when putting this one together—you need to think about what it will look like when it's flipped over. You can lay the pear pieces out in a fancy, overlapping pattern or get rustic as, I have here, by placing whole pear halves round-side up so that they look like jewels studding the gingerbread. Serve with Caramel Sauce (page 305) and Crème Fraîche (page 302) or Vanilla (page 230) or Salted Caramel Ice Cream (page 232).

½ cup	unsalted butter	125 mL
1½ cups	granulated sugar	375 mL
5	pears, peeled, halved, and cored	5
1 cup	all-purpose flour	250 mL
1 tbsp	ground ginger	15 mL
1 tsp	ground cinnamon	5 mL
¼ tsp	ground nutmeg	1 mL
¼ tsp	ground cloves	1 mL
2	large free-range egg yolks	2
¼ cup	dark molasses	60 mL
6 tbsp	unsalted butter	90 mL
2 tbsp	packed golden brown sugar	30 mL
¼ cup	corn syrup	60 mL
1 tsp	baking soda	5 mL
2 tbsp	brewed strong coffee, boiling hot	30 mL
4	large free-range egg whites	4
2 tbsp	granulated sugar	30 mL

1. In a large heavy skillet or sauté pan, over low heat, combine butter and sugar and cook until mixture starts to turn a medium amber color. Remove from heat. Very slowly and carefully (moist fruit will cause the butter mixture to split), place pear halves in the pan in a single layer. Return to low heat. Cook pears, turning as needed, until caramelized and tender enough to easily pierce with a fork. Transfer pears to a plate to cool. Reserve caramel to serve with cake.

2. Arrange cooled pears in a 9-inch (23 cm) round cake pan: 8 pear halves around the outside edge with narrow ends facing toward the center and 2 pear halves filling in the center.

3. In a large bowl, sift together flour, ginger, cinnamon, nutmeg, and cloves. Set aside.

continued . . .

4. In a small bowl, combine egg yolks and molasses. Set aside.
5. In a mixing bowl, using an electric mixer on medium-high speed, beat butter until soft peaks form. Beat in brown sugar. At low speed, beat in one-third of the dry ingredients and then one-half of the egg yolk mixture. Repeat. Dissolve baking soda in coffee and beat into mixture. Beat in last one-third of dry ingredients.
6. In a separate bowl, whisk egg whites until soft peaks form. Add sugar and whisk until shiny. Spoon over arranged pears in pan.
7. Spoon batter over pears. Bake in preheated oven for 18 to 20 minutes, or until a wooden skewer inserted in the middle comes out clean. Remove from oven and set aside to cool in pan for 10 minutes.
8. Place a large round platter face down over the cake pan. Holding both firmly, invert the pan to release the cake onto the platter.

almond cake with strawberries and raspberry coulis

makes one 8-inch (20 cm) cake

If you're an almond lover like me, you're going to be making this dessert a lot. It's very easy to make and goes with just about everything. If strawberries aren't in season, try blackberries, blueberries, huckleberries, or even roasted peaches.

tips

Almond paste can be bought from specialty stores or bakeries, but it is easy to make yourself (see page 319).

You can substitute Kirsch, Grand Marnier, or water for the Cointreau.

You want this cake to be very moist, so keep an eye on it near the end of the bake time: it should be just barely set in the middle when you pull it out of the oven.

This cake can be made the day before and kept covered. It is my go-to cake in the summer, as it goes with just about every fruit, from berries to sliced nectarines, plums, mango, cherries, or pineapple. I like to macerate the fruit in a little honey and liquor for 30 minutes to 1 hour before serving.

⅓ cup	cake flour	75 mL
½ tsp	baking powder	2.5 mL
¼ tsp	fine sea salt	1 mL
¾ cup	granulated sugar	175 mL
½ cup	salted butter, softened	125 mL
7 oz	almond paste	210 g
3	large free-range eggs	3
1 tbsp	Cointreau	15 mL
½ tsp	pure almond extract	2.5 mL
•	Confectioners' (icing) sugar	•
1½ cups	heavy or whipping (35%) cream, whipped to soft peaks	375 mL
1½ cups	fresh strawberries, hulled and quartered	375 mL
•	Raspberry Coulis (page 298)	•

1. Preheat oven to 350°F (180°C). Butter and flour an 8-inch (20 cm) springform pan.
2. In a small bowl, sift together flour, baking powder, and salt. Set aside.
3. In a mixing bowl, using an electric mixer on medium-high speed, mix sugar and butter until light and fluffy. Add almond paste, a bit at a time, and mix until combined. Add eggs one at a time and mix until combined. Add Cointreau and almond extract and mix until combined. Carefully add dry ingredients and mix until just combined.
4. Pour batter into prepared springform pan. Bake in preheated oven for 30 to 35 minutes, or until golden and just barely set in the middle. Remove from oven and cool completely in pan. Remove from pan and dust with confectioners' sugar.
5. To serve, slice cake and place on individual serving plates. Top with a dollop of cream. Drizzle with raspberry coulis and add a spoonful of strawberries.

concord cake à la notre

makes 12 servings

This cake looks like New Year's Eve on a plate but is really easy to put together. If you are nervous about making meringue, do not be daunted: the key is to whip the meringue until it holds a lovely, glossy sheen and all of the sugar has been dissolved. Putting this one together is really fun. The meringue "sticks" are very forgiving when assembling the cake. You just stick them in the mousse whichever way you see fit. Dust with a little cocoa and confectioner's sugar and you'll be sure to impress.

meringues

2 cups	confectioners' (icing) sugar	500 mL
7 tbsp	unsweetened cocoa powder	105 mL
10	large free-range egg whites (about 1¼ cups/300 mL)	10
1⅓ cup	granulated sugar	325 mL

mousse

6	large free-range eggs, separated	6
2½ tbsp	granulated sugar	37 mL
8 oz	70% bittersweet (dark) chocolate	250 g
½ cup	unsalted butter	125 mL
•	Confectioners' (icing) sugar	•

1. Preheat oven to 250°F (120°C). Butter and lightly flour a baking sheet or line with parchment paper. Using a pencil, draw three 9- by 5½-inch (23 by 13.5 cm) ovals on the parchment paper as a piping guide. Turn the paper over.
2. MAKE MERINGUES: In a medium bowl, sift together cocoa and confectioners' sugar. Set aside.
3. In a mixing bowl, using an electric mixer on medium-high speed, beat egg whites until firm, adding 3 tbsp (45 mL) granulated sugar halfway through. As soon as egg whites are stiff, reduce to low speed and beat in remaining sugar. Using a wooden spatula, quickly fold in dry ingredients. Gently spoon about 2 cups (500 mL) into a pastry bag fitted with #4 or ½-inch (1 cm) plain tip. Starting in the center of oval on the prepared baking sheet, pipe the meringue in a spiral pattern out to the penciled border. Repeat on other 2 ovals. Gently spoon remaining meringue into pastry bag. Pipe into long strips the length of the baking sheet. Bake in preheated oven for 1 hour and 15 minutes, or until

continued . . .

firm and dry. After 15 minutes of baking, check color of meringues. They should not brown. If they are beginning to color, lower the heat. When done, meringues are hard and easily removed from the baking sheet. Remove from oven to cool. Set aside.

4. MAKE MOUSSE: In a nonreactive bowl set over a saucepan of simmering water (make sure water does not touch bottom of bowl), melt chocolate. Remove from heat, add butter, and stir until the mixture reaches the consistency of very thick cream. Set aside to cool completely. Once cool, stir in egg yolks, one at a time.

5. In a mixing bowl, using an electric mixer on medium-high speed, beat egg whites until very stiff, adding sugar halfway through. Fold in chocolate mixture.

6. ASSEMBLE: On a cardboard cake board or a flat plate, place 1 meringue oval and cover it with one-quarter of the mousse. Repeat. Place last meringue oval and cover top and sides with remaining half of the mousse. Break meringue strips into 1- and 2-inch (2.5 to 5 cm) sticks (the sizes should be a bit irregular as it looks much better that way). Randomly cover top and sides of cake with meringue pieces. Refrigerate for 1 hour. Sprinkle with icing sugar before serving.

tip

If you are able make the meringues 1 or 2 days in advance, leave the meringue in the oven overnight with the heat turned off. This really dries the meringue out, and is especially important if you live in a damp or humid climate (moisture is the enemy of meringue).

white-chocolate pistachio gâteau

makes one 9-inch (23 cm) cake

White chocolate and pistachios are a match made in heaven. Not only is the color combination gorgeous, but the creamy cocoa butter perfectly balances the nuttiness of the pistachios. And this cake is feather-light: a thin sponge base is topped with white-chocolate mousse and decorated with white-chocolate curls. Beautiful and delicious.

sponge

¾ cup	all-purpose flour	175 mL
½ cup	granulated sugar	125 mL
¼ cup	finely ground pistachios	60 mL
½ tsp	baking soda	2.5 mL
¼ tsp	fine sea salt	1 mL
¼ cup	vegetable oil	60 mL
½ cup	freshly squeezed orange juice	125 mL
1 tbsp	freshly squeezed lemon juice	15 mL

filling

12 oz	white chocolate	375 g
¾ cup	heavy or whipping (35%) cream	175 mL
1½ tsp	gelatin	7 mL
3 tbsp	water	45 mL
½ cup	chopped pistachios, toasted	125 mL
1½ cups	Additional heavy or whipping (35%) cream	375 mL

• White-chocolate curls and confectioners' (icing) sugar OR Whipped cream and fresh berries •

continued . . .

1. Preheat oven to 350°F (180°C). Butter a 9-inch (23 cm) springform pan. Line bottom with a circle of parchment paper and then butter paper.

2. MAKE SPONGE: In a large bowl, combine flour, sugar, pistachios, baking soda, and salt.

3. In another bowl, whisk together oil, orange juice, and lemon juice. Pour the wet ingredients into the dry ingredients and stir until well combined (be careful not to overmix). Pour into prepared springform pan. Bake in preheated oven for 15 to 18 minutes, or until a toothpick inserted comes out dry. Remove pan from oven and place on a wire rack to cool completely.

4. MAKE FILLING: Meanwhile, in a bowl set over a saucepan of simmering water (make sure water does not touch bottom of bowl), melt chocolate with ¾ cup (175 mL) cream, stirring constantly until chocolate is completely melted and mixture is smooth. Remove pan from the heat and set aside.

5. Dissolve gelatin in a small bowl of water. Stir into melted chocolate along with the nuts. Set aside to cool to room temperature.

6. In a mixing bowl, using an electric mixer on medium-high speed, whip 1½ cups (375 mL) cream to soft peaks. Fold into chocolate mixture. Pour over the sponge base in the springform pan. Cover and refrigerate overnight, or for at least 3 hours.

7. SERVE: Run a sharp knife between the cake and the inside of the pan. Remove the springform pan ring. Garnish top of cake with white-chocolate curls and confectioners' sugar or with whipped cream and fresh berries.

tip

To make white-chocolate curls, place a 1 lb (500 g) block of white chocolate on a plate and microwave on High for 20 to 30 seconds. Using a very sharp vegetable peeler, peel curls off the side of the block. You may find that you'll need to microwave the chocolate a little along the way to get it to the right consistency to peel. (You can also rub the heel of your hand against the chocolate to warm it.) Peel the curls onto a piece of parchment or waxed paper and then mound on the cake.

tips

To finely dust cocoa powder, place it in a small fine-mesh sieve and tap the edge of the sieve slightly while holding it over the cake, being careful to evenly cover the desired areas.

This cake can be made a day or two in advance, stored in an airtight container, and frozen for up to 1 month. To bring back that just-baked texture, just thaw it out and bring to room temperature before popping it in the oven at 325°F (160°C) for 10 minutes.

beijing chocolate spice cake

makes one 9-inch (23 cm) cake

Don't let the simplicity of this single-layer cake fool you. The aromatic spices blended with the chocolate create a depth of flavor that is far from ordinary. In fact, all you need to finish this cake is glaze it with a light ganache. If you want to take it a step further, serve with some Crème Anglaise (page 303), mascarpone, or Crème Fraîche (page 302) alongside. It's sure to impress even the most discerning crowd.

6	large free-range eggs	6
1¼ cups	granulated sugar, divided	300 mL
7 oz	unsweetened chocolate	210 g
6 oz	70% bittersweet (dark) chocolate	175 g
½ cup	water	125 mL
2 tsp	Chinese 5-spice powder	10 mL
½ cup + 2 tbsp	unsalted butter	125 mL + 30 mL
•	Unsweetened Dutch-process cocoa	•

1. Preheat oven to 350°F (180°C). Butter a 9-inch (23 cm) springform pan and wrap around the outside with two layers of aluminum foil. Place springform pan in a baking pan of at least the same depth.
2. In a mixing bowl, using an electric mixer on medium-high speed, beat eggs and ¾ cup (175 mL) sugar together until fluffy and light in color, about 5 minutes. Set aside.
3. Place unsweetened and bittersweet chocolate in a heatproof bowl set over a saucepan of simmering water (make sure water does not touch bottom of bowl) and heat gently, stirring occasionally, until completely melted. (Alternatively, melt in a microwave.)
4. In a medium saucepan over low heat, combine water, remaining ½ cup (125 mL) sugar, and Chinese 5-spice powder and cook, stirring often, until sugar dissolves. Add melted chocolate and stir to combine. Add all of the butter and stir until melted. Working in two or three batches, fold in egg mixture. Pour batter into prepared pan.
5. Bring a kettle of water to boil. Pour the hot water into the baking pan until it reaches halfway up the side of the springform pan. Bake in preheated oven for 40 to 50 minutes, or until the top is set with a slight jiggle in the center. Remove from oven. Carefully lift out of the water bath and place on a wire rack to cool completely. If desired, glaze with Chocolate Ganache (page 307). To serve, slice and dust with cocoa.

variation

For a Mexican twist, substitute the five-spice powder with 1 tsp (5 mL) ground cinnamon and a large pinch of cayenne.

cracker queen's chocolate macadamia nut cake

makes one 9-inch (23 cm) cake

Don't be disturbed when it looks like the center of this cake has fallen—it's supposed to do that! The cake will inflate and then condense back down on itself into a single thick, dense chocolate macadamia layer. You can go ahead and glaze it with ganache if you like, but I prefer to go with something simple yet stunning, so I mound the center with whipped cream and decorate it with Caramel Chunks (page 76).

8 oz	70% bittersweet (dark) chocolate	250 g
1 cup	macadamia nuts, toasted	250 mL
¼ cup + ½ cup + ½ cup	granulated sugar	60 mL + 125 mL + 125 mL
1 cup	unsalted butter	250 mL
8	large free-range eggs, separated	8
½ tsp	fine sea salt	2.5 mL
	glaze	
½ cup	heavy or whipping (35%) cream	125 mL
8 oz	70% bittersweet (dark) chocolate, chopped into small chunks	250 g
1 tbsp	unsalted butter, softened	15 mL
	OR	
1 cup	heavy or whipping (35%) cream, whipped to soft peaks	250 mL
.	Cocoa powder	.

1. Preheat oven to 350°F (180°C). Butter a 9-inch (23 cm) springform pan. Line bottom with a circle of parchment paper and butter the paper.
2. In a bowl set over a saucepan of simmering water (make sure water does not touch bottom of bowl), melt chocolate, stirring often, until smooth. Remove from heat and set aside to cool to room temperature.
3. In a food processor fitted with the metal blade, pulse macadamia nuts and ¼ cup (60 mL) sugar until very fine, like flour. Set aside.
4. In a mixing bowl, using an electric mixer on medium-high speed, beat butter until soft. Add ½ cup (125 mL) sugar and mix well. Add egg yolks, one at a time, beating after each addition until smooth. Slowly add chocolate and beat until well combined. Add macadamia nuts and mix until just combined.

continued . . .

5. In a clean mixing bowl, using an electric mixer on medium-high speed, beat egg whites and salt until soft peaks form. Gradually add the remaining ½ cup (125 mL) sugar and beat until the peaks hold but are not dry or too stiff.

6. Fold one-third of the whites into the chocolate mixture and mix very gently until well combined. Repeat twice more with remaining whites.

7. Pour batter into prepared springform pan. Bake in preheated oven for 45 to 50 minutes, or until the top is dry and firm around the edges but still wobbly in the center (be careful not to over-bake; the center may crack but should remain soft). Remove pan from oven and set aside to cool completely before removing sides from pan.

8. MAKE GLAZE: In a small saucepan over medium heat, bring cream just to a boil. Remove pan from heat and add chocolate. Set aside for 2 to 3 minutes to let chocolate melt, then whisk until smooth. Add butter and whisk to combine.

9. FINISH: Place cake on a serving platter (the sides will be slightly higher than the center). If glazing, trim top so sides are even with the center. Invert cake on platter. Pour glaze over. (If not glazing, no need to trim or invert cake.) Mound whipped cream on top and, if desired, dust with cocoa.

tip

To toast macadamia nuts, arrange in a single layer on a baking sheet and bake in a preheated 325°F (160°C) oven for about 10 minutes. Watch them closely and give the tray a shake halfway through.

chocolate date pecan cake with bourbon crème anglaise

makes one 8-inch (20 cm) cake

Dates are one of nature's greatest sweeteners, and when paired with chocolate they elevate this single-layer cake to something very special. This cake is so good on its own that I never ice it.

⅓ cup	finely chopped pitted Medjool dates	75 mL
⅓ cup	brewed coffee	75 mL
11 oz	70% bittersweet (dark) chocolate	330 g
¾ cup	salted butter	175 mL
¾ cup + ¼ cup	granulated sugar	175 mL + 60 mL
5	large free-range egg yolks	5
4	large free-range egg whites	4
1 cup	pecans, toasted and finely chopped	250 mL
7 tbsp	all-purpose flour	105 mL
·	Confectioners' (icing) sugar	·
·	Bourbon Crème Anglaise (page 303)	·

tip
....
If you don't have bourbon on hand, a good brandy will do nicely.

1. In a small bowl, cover dates with coffee and set aside to soak for at least 1 hour.
2. Preheat oven to 325°F (160°C). Butter an 8-inch (20 cm) springform pan and line base with parchment paper.
3. In a medium heavy-bottomed saucepan over low heat, slowly melt chocolate and butter. Remove from heat and set aside to cool. Once cool, add date mixture and stir to combine.
4. In a mixing bowl, using an electric mixer on medium-high speed, beat ¾ cup (175 mL) sugar and egg yolks until the yolks are pale and thick. Stir in chocolate mixture. Set aside.
5. In a small bowl, toss together pecans and flour. Add pecan mixture to chocolate-yolk mixture and stir to combine.
6. In a clean mixing bowl, using an electric mixer on medium-high speed, beat egg whites to soft peaks. Add remaining ¼ cup (60 mL) sugar and beat for another minute.
7. Gently fold half the egg whites into the chocolate-yolk mixture. When combined, fold in remaining egg whites.
8. Pour batter into prepared springform pan. Bake in preheated oven for 25 to 30 minutes, or until dry and firm but still jiggly in the center (the middle should still be moist). Remove from oven and set aside to cool completely before removing from pan.
9. Invert cake on platter. Dust with confectioners' sugar and offer Bourbon Crème Anglaise alongside.

gâteau progrès with french roast coffee coulis

makes one 9-inch (23 cm) cake

This cake is a chocoholic's dream come true yet is so simple to put together: dark chocolate ganache is sandwiched between two chocolate meringue disks and drizzled with coffee coulis. To make the meringues even in size, draw templates on parchment paper and then use them as a guide when piping the meringue. Rich and decadent, a little of this cake goes a very long way.

Meringue

¾ cup	hazelnuts, toasted	175 mL
¾ cup	blanched slivered almonds, toasted	175 mL
6	large free-range egg whites	6
1 cup	granulated sugar	250 mL

Ganache

1 cup	heavy or whipping (35%) cream	250 mL
12 oz	70% bittersweet (dark) chocolate, finely chopped	375 g
⅛ tsp	orange oil or 1 tbsp (15 mL) Grand Marnier (optional)	0.5 mL

Buttercream

1½ cup	granulated sugar	375 mL
½ cups	water	125 mL
5	large free-range egg whites	5
2 cups	unsalted butter, softened	500 mL
2 tsp	espresso powder dissolved in 1 tbsp (15 mL) hot water, cooled completely	10 mL

Garnish

12	whole hazelnuts, toasted	12
·	Confectioners' (icing) sugar	·

continued . . .

1. Preheat oven 350°F (180°C). Line 3 baking sheets with parchment paper.
2. MAKE MERINGUE: Grind the nuts to a fine powder (be careful not to turn them into paste). Set aside.
3. In a mixing bowl, using an electric mixer on medium-high speed, beat egg whites until soft peaks form. Gradually add sugar and beat until glossy. Carefully fold in ground nuts. Spoon into a large (no. 4) piping bag. Using the base of a 9-inch (23 cm) round baking pan, trace a circle on each piece of parchment paper lining baking sheets. Pipe meringue in a spiral, starting at the middle of the circle.
4. Bake in preheated oven for 1½ hours or until firm. Remove baking sheets from oven and set aside to cool.
5. MAKE GANACHE: In a heavy-bottomed saucepan over medium-low heat, bring cream just to a boil. Remove pan from heat and add chocolate and orange oil (if using). Set aside for 2 to 3 minutes, until the chocolate is completely melted. Whisk until smooth. Reserve ½ cup (125 mL) ganache in piping bag for rosette garnish.
6. MAKE BUTTERCREAM: In a medium heavy-bottomed saucepan, combine sugar and water and bring to a boil. Reduce heat and simmer until it reaches the soft ball stage, which is 240°F (115°C) on a candy thermometer. Remove pan from heat and set aside.
7. In a medium mixing bowl, using an electric mixer on medium-high speed, beat egg whites until soft peaks form. In a slow, steady stream, pour sugar syrup into the egg whites. Beat mixture until cool, about 20 minutes. Slowly beat in butter. Beat in espresso.
8. ASSEMBLE: On a serving platter, place a round of meringue. Spread half of ganache evenly over top. Cover with half of the buttercream. Place another meringue round on top. Repeat with remaining ganache and buttercream. Place the third meringue round on top. Pipe 12 rosettes around the edge of the top meringue. Place a hazelnut on top of each rosette. Dust with icing sugar. Refrigerate until serving. Serve the same day (the meringue gets soft if it is kept overnight).

tips

To remove the skins of the hazelnuts, rub the nuts against a fine-mesh metal sieve.

For the best presentation, cut servings using a very sharp knife.

dinner
party
desserts

for best results

This is the chapter where we really go to town. Here I include recipes that are not necessarily more difficult, but rather have more than one component to dress them up. From cobbler to panna cotta to sticky toffee pudding, these desserts are often partnered with a sauce, coulis, or ice cream for spectacular results, and they are the desserts I serve to friends and family. Almost all of these desserts can be made ahead of time, which is crucial when you are having a dinner party.

01 · Don't let dessert be an afterthought. Plan it at the same time that you are considering your entrée.

02 · Don't stack your menu with dishes that require a lot of last-minute preparation. For example, a nice risotto followed by Summer Berry Gratin with Champagne Sabayon might go well together, but they both require last-minute preparation that will keep you hidden in the kitchen.

03 · A simple dessert can be elevated to fantastic with the right accompaniment. See the chapter on Toppings and Special Touches (pages 290–311) for inspiration. I always have 2 or 3 sauces on hand, which many sound extravagant or over the top, but they are all easy to make and most can be frozen.

04 · Don't be afraid to serve some fabulous fresh seasonal fruit with crème anglaise or Greek yogurt and a homemade cookie at your next dinner party. Just be sure to warm the cookies before you serve them (who doesn't adore a warm cookie?).

05 · If you are making ice cream, make it the day before or first thing in the morning so it has ample time to firm up.

06 · Use dinner-size (not salad or dessert) plates to serve your creation. It is much more effective for presentation and easier to eat. Who wants the semifreddo sliding off the plate?

07 · Depending on the dessert you are serving (warm or cold), chill or heat your plates slightly for serving.

08 · Invest in a set of ramekins for panna cotta, pots de crème, and individual cobblers or crisps. It looks restaurant-quality and actually makes serving desserts easier (no scooping or cutting).

09 · Store confectioners' sugar and cocoa powder with a small fine-mesh sieve in airtight containers in your pantry. Nothing finishes a dessert like a dusting of one or both of these.

cookie leaves with lemon cream
and passion fruit syrup

makes 1½ dozen cookies

This is a twist on a traditional mille-feuille and one of the desserts I reach for whenever I want something special and sweet yet light and unobtrusive. It's really easy to put together after the main meal while your guests are relaxing between courses. If you have everything ready to go, it's just a matter of stacking and layering for a pretty presentation. Finishing with edible flowers is a simple yet elegant touch.

cookies

⅓ cup	all-purpose flour	75 mL
⅓ cup	granulated sugar	75 mL
¼ cup	unsalted butter, melted	60 mL
2	large free-range egg whites	2
•	Flaked almonds (optional)	•

passion fruit syrup

1 cup	granulated sugar	250 mL
•	Juice of 6 to 8 fresh passion fruits, strained	•
•	Lemon Curd (page 300)	•
•	Whipped cream (½ cup/125 mL per serving)	•
•	Confectioners' (icing) sugar	•
•	Fresh mint, lemon balm, or edible flowers	•

tips

The lemon curd, cookies, and passion fruit syrup can be made up to 3 days in advance. Assemble just before serving.

You can substitute raspberry coulis (page 298) for the passion fruit syrup, and fresh berries for the lemon curd. You can also flavor the whipped cream with 1 tsp (5 mL) Grand Marnier per serving.

1. MAKE COOKIES: In a medium bowl, combine flour and sugar. Stir in melted butter. Slowly incorporate egg whites until smooth. Cover and refrigerate until chilled, at least 2 hours.
2. Preheat oven to 200°F (100°C). Line 2 baking sheets with parchment paper.
3. Remove batter from refrigerator. Spread 1 tsp (5 mL) of batter for each cookie on prepared baking sheets, spaced about 2 inches (5 cm) apart. Sprinkle with almonds (if using). Bake in preheated oven for 2 to 3 minutes, or until lightly golden. Remove from oven and cool on baking sheets for 5 minutes before turning out onto a wire rack to cool completely.
4. MAKE SYRUP: Meanwhile, in a medium saucepan over medium heat, bring sugar and passion fruit juice to a boil and continue boiling, stirring occasionally, just until sugar dissolves. Remove from heat. Set aside to cool.
5. ASSEMBLE: Take one cookie and spread 2 tbsp (30 mL) lemon curd on top. Place a second cookie on top and spread ½ cup (125 mL) whipped cream on it. Finish with a third cookie. Dust with confectioners' sugar. Repeat with remaining cookies.
6. SERVE: Swirl a generous spoonful of passion fruit syrup on each serving plate and place assembled cookie on top. Garnish with mint, lemon balm, or edible flowers.

summer berry gratin with cointreau sabayon sauce

makes 6 servings

This traditional French summer dessert can be prepared using any type of fruit, but is especially lovely when made with fresh, ripe seasonal berries. The berries aren't actually cooked, but rather warmed to bring out their flavors; the sabayon is quickly browned overtop them. Have all of the components ready, measured, and at hand—this recipe moves really quickly once it gets rolling. You need 10 minutes of concentrated time to complete this recipe, which is just enough time between courses.

8	large free-range egg yolks	8
1 cup	sparkling white wine	250 mL
¼ cup + 2 tbsp	Cointreau	60 mL + 30 mL
½ cup	granulated sugar	125 mL
Generous 2 cups	berries (raspberries, blueberries, blackberries, red or black currants, or any combination)	Generous 500 mL

tip

For a family-style presentation, make this in a casserole dish rather than in individual serving bowls.

1. In a medium heatproof bowl, combine egg yolks, wine, Cointreau, and sugar. Set over a saucepan of simmering water (make sure water does not touch bottom of bowl) and whisk constantly until mixture forms thick, frothy, pale ribbons, 4 to 6 minutes.
2. Turn oven on to broil and place a rack in the top position.
3. Divide berries among 6 individual gratin (or shallow, ovenproof) dishes. Spoon sauce over berries. Arrange dishes on a baking sheet and broil for 1 to 2 minutes, or just until top is slightly golden. Serve immediately.

pavlova with honey basil nectarines, almond cream, and salty caramel

makes 1 pavlova

Summer stone fruits are such a sight for sore eyes when they finally hit the market stands. Here I've chosen fresh nectarines as a topping for a traditional pavlova and paired them with some fragrant basil and sweet honey. Don't be daunted by this classic dessert. I promise you'll be surprised by how easy it is to prepare. Be sure to let the nectarines macerate in the honey for a few minutes—this will allow the fruits to release some of their juices and create a wonderful, syrupy sauce. This is our daughter Gillian's favourite dessert to make—it always wows everyone.

1½ cups	granulated sugar	375 mL
4 tsp	cornstarch	20 mL
¾ cup	large free-range egg whites	175 mL
Pinch	fine sea salt	Pinch
2 tsp	white vinegar	10 mL
½ tsp	pure vanilla extract	2.5 mL
8	ripe nectarines, pitted and cut into sixth or eighths (depending on size)	8
10	fresh basil leaves	10
¼ cup	freshly squeezed lemon juice	60 mL
¼ cup	liquid honey	60 mL
1 tsp	ground cinnamon	5 mL
2 cups	heavy or whipping (35%) cream	500 mL
1 tsp	pure almond extract	5 mL
•	Caramel Sauce (page 305)	•
•	Fleur de sel (or other flaky sea salt)	•

1. Preheat oven to 250°F (120°C). Line a baking sheet with parchment paper.
2. In a medium bowl, sift together sugar and cornstarch. Set aside.
3. In a mixing bowl, using an electric mixer on medium-high speed, beat egg whites and salt until soft peaks form. Gradually add sugar mixture while mixing. Add vinegar and vanilla. Beat on high speed for 5 minutes, until extra thick and glossy. Mound individual meringues, 3 tbsp (45 mL) at a time, about 2 inches (5 cm) apart, or 1 large round meringue, on prepared baking sheet. Make a small indent in the center of each individual mound, or a medium-sized indent

continued . . .

tip

See my YouTube video on how to make pavlova.

in a large meringue, so meringue resembles a nest. Bake in preheated oven for 1 hour. Turn oven off and leave meringue(s) in oven for another hour. Remove pan from oven and set aside to cool completely before removing meringues from baking sheet.

4. In another bowl, toss nectarines with basil, lemon juice, honey, and cinnamon. Set aside for a few minutes to macerate.

5. In a clean mixing bowl, using an electric mixer on medium-high speed, whip cream and almond extract until soft peaks form.

6. To serve, fill center of meringue with whipped cream and top with prepared nectarines. Drizzle with caramel sauce and sprinkle with sea salt flakes.

variations

01. This dessert is a show-stopper (see the cover of this book) and can be adapted for most summer fruits. I will often mix ½ cup (125 mL) lemon curd (page 300) into the whipped cream meringue topping and top with fresh blueberries, raspberries, or blackberries (or all three) and skip the caramel sauce.

02. For another divine interpretation, make individual meringues and fill with ice cream (homemade or best-quality store bought) and drizzle with warm Chocolate Ganache (page 307) and Hazelnut Praline (page 311).

caramelized pears with brown-butter ice cream and french brandy snaps

makes 6 servings

This is one of my favorite desserts when the colder months roll around. I love the way the temperatures and textures of the pears and ice cream play off each other. As with most simple desserts, the better the ingredients, the better the flavors, so if you aren't making your own ice cream, be sure to buy the best quality you can get.

4	firm, ripe pears	4
2 tbsp	freshly squeezed lemon juice	30 mL
¼ cup	unsalted butter	60 mL
½ cup	granulated sugar	125 mL
.	Vanilla Ice Cream (page 230)	.
.	French Brandy Snaps with Almonds (page 256)	.

1. Peel pears and cut lengthwise into 6 wedges, discarding cores.
2. In a medium bowl, toss pears with lemon juice.
3. In a heavy-bottomed sauté pan or skillet large enough to hold the pears in a single layer, over low heat, melt butter. Add pears and cook for 3 minutes, shaking pan occasionally. Sprinkle pears with sugar and cook for another 3 to 5 minutes, shaking the pan and turning the pears until sugar is melted and pears are tender and slightly golden.
4. To serve, in individual serving bowls, place a large scoop of ice cream and top with caramelized pears. Arrange a brandy snap upright in the ice cream. Serve immediately.

tip

Choose Anjou or Bosc pears for
this dessert as they will soften but
still keep their shape when cooked
(avoid Bartletts: they will give off
too much juice). It is definitely worth
trying with other heirloom varieties
you might find at your local farmers'
market or in your own backyard.

cherry clafoutis with amaretto and crème fraîche

makes 6 servings

A French dessert, clafoutis is a cross between a soufflé and a pancake. Cherries are the traditional fruit of choice, and I love how they burst when you bite into them, but you can use whatever fruit you have on hand with good results. And if there's any left over from your dinner party, this dish is lovely with nice cup of coffee the morning after.

3	large free-range eggs	3
¾ cup	heavy or whipping (35%) cream	175 mL
¾ cup	whole milk	175 mL
1 tbsp	amaretto	15 mL
6 tbsp	all-purpose flour	90 mL
½ cup + 3 tbsp	granulated sugar	125 mL + 45 mL
Pinch	fine sea salt	Pinch
½	plump vanilla bean, split open	½
2 tbsp	unsalted butter	30 mL
3 cups	pitted cherries	750 mL
·	Confectioners' (icing) sugar	·
½ cup	Crème Fraîche (page 302)	125 mL

1. In a mixing bowl, on medium-high speed, beat eggs until frothy. Add cream, milk, and amaretto and mix until well combined.
2. In a medium bowl, combine flour, sugar, and salt. Using a knife, scrape the seeds out of the vanilla bean into the flour. Gradually add egg-milk mixture to the flour mixture and whisk to combine. Set aside for 10 minutes to rest.
3. Preheat oven to 350°F (180°C). Butter and sugar an 8-cup (2 L) gratin dish.
4. Meanwhile, in a heavy-bottomed sauté pan over medium-low heat, combine butter and sugar and cook, stirring continuously, until sugar has completely dissolved. Add cherries and toss just until the juices from the cherries start to run, 1 to 2 minutes.
5. Using a slotted spoon, spoon cherries into the prepared gratin dish (reserve juice for another use—it's lovely added to sparkling wine or water). Pour the prepared batter over the cherries. Bake in preheated oven for 30 to 40 minutes, until the batter puffs up around the cherries and turns golden brown. Serve warm or at room temperature dusted with confectioners' sugar and with a dollop of crème fraîche.

blueberry cinnamon sugar cobbler

makes one 9-inch (23 cm) cobbler

I know that for many people peach cobbler is a summertime staple, but being from British Columbia and surrounded by an assortment of fresh fruit, I love to mix things up and bake with whatever is freshest and in season. Blueberries are one of my summer favorites, and they are perfect in this cobbler. Serve warm with a scoop of ice cream—Vanilla (page 230), lemon, or Salted Caramel Ice Cream (page 232) would all be lovely.

4 cups	fresh blueberries	1 L
2 tsp	grated lemon zest	10 mL
2 tsp	freshly squeezed lemon juice	10 mL
2 tbsp	packed golden brown sugar	30 mL
2 tsp + 1½ cups	all-purpose flour	10 mL + 375 mL
2 tbsp	granulated sugar	30 mL
1 tsp	baking powder	5 mL
¼ tsp	fine sea salt	1 mL
½ tsp	ground cinnamon	2.5 mL
6 tbsp	cold butter, cut into 1-inch (2.5 cm) cubes	90 mL
⅔ cup	heavy or whipping (35%) cream, cold	150 mL
1	large free-range egg, beaten	1
·	Coarse (sanding) sugar	·

tip

You can find coarse sugar in the baking section of most good grocery stores. If you can't get your hands on any, use demerara sugar.

1. Preheat oven to 350°F (180°C).
2. In a bowl, combine blueberries, lemon zest and juice, brown sugar and 2 tsp (10 mL) flour. Transfer to a 9-inch (23 cm) oval gratin dish.
3. In a large bowl, sift together 1½ cups (375 mL) flour, sugar, baking powder, salt, and cinnamon. Using a pastry cutter, cut in butter until mixture is the consistency of coarse sand. Gradually add cream, stirring until dough comes together.
4. On a lightly floured surface, roll out dough to 1-inch (2.5 cm) thickness. Using a cookie cutter or an inverted glass lightly dipped in flour, cut 2½-inch (6 cm) rounds. Arrange on top of blueberries, covering the whole surface. Brush top of dough with beaten egg and sprinkle heavily with the coarse sugar. Bake in preheated oven for 25 to 40 minutes, or until blueberries are bubbling and top is golden. Remove from oven and serve warm.

rhubarb crumble with vanilla semifreddo

makes one 13- by 9-inch (33 by 23 cm) crumble

Making a crumble is one of the nicest ways to enjoy the fruits of summer, and I think the tartness of rhubarb and the sweetness of streusel topping are a perfect combination, but you can swap out the rhubarb for any other fruits with fantastic results.

crumble

12 tbsp	unsalted butter, cut into ½-inch (1 cm) cubes	180 mL
1 cup	sliced almonds	250 mL
1 cup	packed golden brown sugar	250 mL
1¼ tsp	ground cinnamon	6 mL
1¼ cups	all-purpose flour	300 mL

filling

6 cups	fresh rhubarb, cut into ½-inch (1 cm) slices	1.5 L
1½ cups	granulated sugar	375 mL
½ cup + 2 tbsp	all-purpose flour	125 mL + 30 mL
2 tsp	finely grated lemon zest	10 mL

Vanilla Semifreddo (page 220)

Vanilla Semifreddo (page 220)

tips

I love making this dessert in individual (1 cup/250 mL) ramekins.

The streusel topping in this recipe is so good, I usually double it and store half in an airtight container in the freezer so I can whip up a dessert on short notice (which seems to happen a lot at our house over the summer).

1. MAKE CRUMBLE: In a large skillet over medium heat, cook butter until golden, about 5 minutes, stirring often. Remove from heat and stir in almonds, sugar, and cinnamon. Add flour and stir until moist clumps form. Set aside to cool completely.
2. Preheat oven to 350°F (180°C).
3. MAKE FILLING: In a large bowl, toss rhubarb with sugar, flour, and lemon zest. Let stand until filling looks moist, stirring a couple of times.
4. ASSEMBLE: Pour filling into a 13- x 9-inch (33 by 23 cm) gratin dish. Sprinkle crumble evenly over top. Bake in preheated oven for 45 to 60 minutes, or until filling is bubbling and crumble is crisp and golden. Remove pan from oven and set aside to cool for 10 to 15 minutes. Serve warm or at room temperature with a scoop of Vanilla Semifreddo.

ginger coconut macadamia nut shortcakes with warm peaches and cream

makes 8 individual shortcakes

This is a fun variation on classic strawberry shortcake. You'll love the tropical flavors. If macadamia nuts are hard to come by, almonds will work just as well.

shortcakes

1½ cup	all-purpose flour	375 mL
2¼ tsp	baking powder	11 mL
1 tbsp	granulated sugar	15 mL
1 tsp	fine sea salt	5 mL
6 tbsp	cold unsalted butter, cut into ½-inch (1 cm) cubes	90 mL
⅓ cup	candied ginger, cut into small chunks	75 mL
⅓ cup	unsweetened thread coconut	75 mL
½ cup	roughly chopped macadamia nuts, toasted	125 mL
¾ cup	heavy or whipping (35%) cream	175 mL
1	large free-range egg, beaten	1
•	Coarse (sanding) sugar	•

peaches

4	ripe peaches	4
2 tbsp	unsalted butter	30 mL
3 tbsp	packed golden brown sugar	45 mL
1 tbsp	freshly squeezed lemon juice	15 mL
1½ cups	heavy or whipping (35%) cream, whipped to soft peaks	375 mL
•	Confectioners' (icing) sugar	•

tip

You can find coarse sugar in the baking section of most good grocery stores. If you can't get your hands on any, use demerara sugar.

1. Preheat oven to 375°F (190°C). Line a baking sheet with parchment paper.
2. MAKE SHORTCAKES: In a large bowl, combine flour, baking powder, sugar, and salt. Add butter cubes and stir to coat with flour. Using a pastry cutter, cut butter into very small (pea-sized) pieces. Working quickly, blend with your fingers until mixture is the consistency of coarse sand. Stir in ginger, coconut, and nuts. Stir in cream until just combined.

continued . . .

3. On a lightly floured surface, roll out dough to 1½-inch (4 cm) thickness.

4. Using a cookie cutter or an inverted glass lightly dipped in flour, cut into 3½-inch (8.5 cm) rounds. Transfer to prepared baking sheet, spaced 1½ inches (4 cm) apart. Brush with beaten egg and sprinkle with sugar. Bake in preheated oven for 10 to 12 minutes, or until slightly golden. Remove from oven and cool on baking sheet for 5 to 10 minutes before turning out onto a wire rack to cool completely.

5. MAKE PEACHES: Half fill a large bowl with cold water and ice. Bring a large saucepan of water to a boil. Using a sharp knife, score the bottom (opposite the stem end) of each peach with an X. Place the peaches in the boiling water for about 1 minute. Using a slotted spoon, transfer peaches to the ice water. When peaches are cool enough to handle, starting at the X, use a sharp paring knife to peel off the skin (the skin should peel off easily). Cut each peach off the pit into 6 wedges.

6. In a medium sauté pan over medium heat, melt butter. Add sugar and cook, stirring constantly, for 1 minute. Add lemon juice and cook, stirring constantly, until sugar dissolves. Add peach wedges. Toss to coat and warm through.

7. ASSEMBLE: Cut each shortcake in half horizontally. On the bottom half of the shortcake, spoon some peaches and then a generous dollop of whipped cream. Cover with the top half of the shortcake. Place on an individual serving plate. Dust with confectioners' sugar.

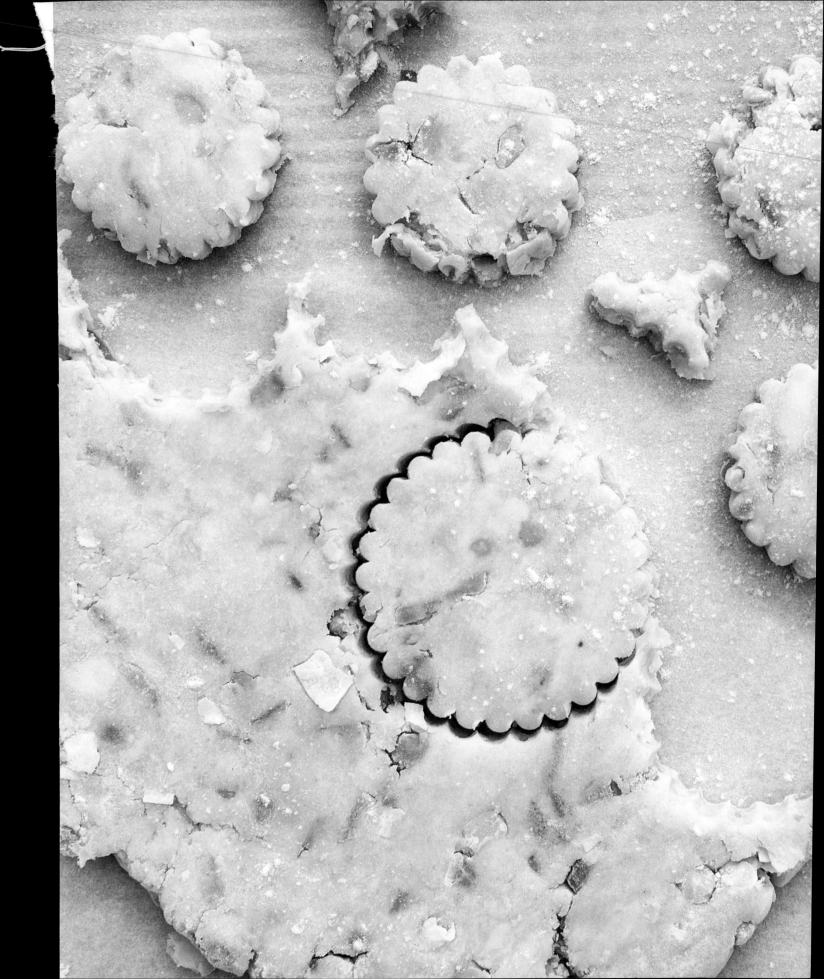

toasted coconut bread with date and bourbon semifreddo and butterscotch sauce

makes 1 loaf

Individually, the components of this dish are delicious. Combined, they're extraordinary. Comforting and rich, this is the perfect dessert to serve a crowd after barbecued burgers or ribs.

coconut bread

1 cup	all-purpose flour	250 mL
1 tsp	baking powder	5 mL
½ tsp	baking soda	2.5 mL
⅓ cup	unsalted butter	75 mL
⅔ cup	granulated sugar	150 mL
2	large free-range eggs	2
1 tsp	pure almond extract	5 mL
3 tbsp	2% milk	45 mL
1 cup	mashed ripe banana	250 mL
1 cup + ¼ cup	unsweetened flaked coconut	250 mL + 60 mL
½ cup	chopped pecans, toasted	125 mL

•	Date and Bourbon Semifreddo (page 225)	•
•	Butterscotch Sauce (page 306)	•

1. Preheat oven to 350°F (180°C). Butter a 8- by 4- by 2½-inch (20 by 10 by 6 cm) loaf pan and line with parchment paper.
2. MAKE BREAD: In a large bowl, sift together flour, baking powder, baking soda, and salt. Set aside.
3. In a mixing bowl, using an electric mixer, beat butter and sugar until light and fluffy. In alternating batches, add dry ingredients and banana and mix until just combined. Fold in 1 cup (250 mL) coconut and pecans. Pour batter into prepared loaf pan. Top with remaining ¼ cup (60 mL) coconut. Bake in preheated oven for 35 to 45 minutes, or until a toothpick inserted into the middle comes out clean. Remove pan from oven and place on a wire rack to cool completely. Once cool, cut loaf into 1-inch (2.5 cm) slices.
4. ASSEMBLE: On individual serving plates, arrange 1 slice with a scoop of ice cream. Drizzle with a spoonful of warm butterscotch sauce and serve immediately.

white-chocolate brioche pudding with port and dried cherry sauce

makes 10 to 12 servings

This isn't your average, stodgy bread pudding: this version brings comfort food to a whole new level. A base of rich brioche mixed with white chocolate and drizzled with a dried cherry sauce. Even those who say they don't like white chocolate will love this dessert.

brioche pudding

1	loaf brioche or challah	1
½ cup	granulated sugar	125 mL
7	large free-range egg yolks	7
2	large free-range eggs	2
2 tsp	pure vanilla extract	10 mL
3 cups	heavy or whipping (35%) cream	750 mL
1 cup	2% milk	250 mL
10 oz	white chocolate, chopped	300 g

port and dried cherry sauce

2 cups	port	500 mL
¾ cup	sugar	175 mL
1	2-inch (5 cm) piece cinnamon stick	1
½ cup	dried cherries	125 mL

1. Preheat oven to 350°F (180°C). Butter a 13- by 9-inch (33 by 23 cm) gratin dish.
2. MAKE PUDDING: Trim off ends of the brioche and reserve for other use. Slice remaining loaf into 1-inch (2.5 cm) thick slices (you should have 6 or 7 slices). Cut slices diagonally into triangles. Place on a baking sheet and toast in preheated oven for 2 to 3 minutes, turning once, or until lightly golden on both sides. Remove from oven and cool on baking sheet. When cool, arrange in prepared gratin dish with pointed ends standing up.
3. In a large bowl, whisk together sugar, egg yolks, eggs, and vanilla.
4. In a heavy-bottomed saucepan over medium-low heat, bring cream and milk just to a boil. Remove from heat and add chocolate. Set aside for 2 to 3 minutes, until chocolate melts. Whisk until well combined.

continued . . .

5. Pour ¼ cup (60 mL) of the milk mixture into the egg mixture and whisk to combine. Add remaining milk mixture and whisk to combine. Slowly pour mixture over brioche in gratin dish.

6. Set water to boil. Place gratin dish in a slightly larger baking pan. Pour enough boiling water into the larger pan to come one-third of the way up the side of the gratin dish. Cover with foil, crimping tightly around the edge of the baking pan. Bake in preheated oven for 35 to 45 minutes, or until set and slightly golden. If it isn't golden, remove foil and bake a few minutes longer to allow top to brown slightly. Remove from oven. Transfer gratin dish from pan of water to wire rack to cool. (Cake can be served warm or at room temperature.)

7. MAKE SAUCE: Meanwhile, in a heavy-bottomed saucepan over medium heat, combine port, sugar, and cinnamon and simmer until reduced by half. Discard cinnamon and add cherries. Simmer until cherries are soft. Remove pan from heat and transfer warm sauce to a serving bowl to serve alongside brioche pudding. Will keep in an airtight container in the refrigerator for several months.

tip
....
This dessert can be made the day before up to the end of step 6 and refrigerated overnight. Make sure you remove it from the fridge 1 hour before baking, as it should be brought to room temperature first. Alternatively, allow an extra 15 to 20 minutes of baking time.

coconut pots de crème with toasted coconut chips and pine nut praline

makes 8 servings

People often steer clear of making pot de crème because it needs to be cooked in a water bath (or bain-marie), but don't let this deter you. It's actually very simple and merely requires a little planning. Just be sure to fill your pan no more than one-third full of water, as you don't want the water to bubble up and ruin your custard. Once you get the swing of it, this delicious dessert is one you'll return to again and again, I promise.

6 tbsp	unsalted butter	90 mL
¾ cup	packed golden brown sugar	175 mL
½ tsp	fine sea salt	2.5 mL
1 cup	coconut cream	250 mL
2 cups	heavy or whipping (35%) cream	500 mL
6	large free-range egg yolks	6
1½ cups	heavy or whipping (35%) cream, whipped to soft peaks	375 mL
½ cup	coconut chips, or unsweetened ribbon coconut, toasted	125 mL
•	Pine nut praline (see step 6)	•

1. Preheat oven to 275°F (140°C).
2. In a medium heavy-bottomed saucepan over low heat, melt butter. Stir in sugar and salt and cook until sugar dissolves. Stir in coconut cream and heavy cream and bring just to a boil. Remove from heat and set aside.
3. In a medium bowl, whisk egg yolks. Add ¼ cup (60 mL) of the hot cream mixture and whisk to combine. Whisking continuously, gradually add about 1 cup (250 mL) more of hot cream mixture. Add the yolk-cream mixture in the bowl to the hot cream in the saucepan. Return saucepan to stovetop, on medium-low heat. Stirring constantly, cook until mixture thickens slightly (it should coat the back of a spoon).
4. Strain mixture through a fine-mesh sieve into a heatproof bowl. Discard solids in sieve.

continued . . .

tip
....

The key to a smooth, creamy pot de crème is cooking it over low heat; otherwise it can curdle and you will end up with something resembling sweet scrambled eggs.

variation

You can change the flavor of the pot de crème to vanilla by replacing the coconut cream with whole milk and adding 1½ tsp (7 mL) pure vanilla extract to the milk and cream when you are warming it.

5. Set water to boil. Place 8 ramekins into a baking pan. Pour the mixture into the ramekins. Pour enough boiling water into the baking pan to come one-third of the way up the sides of the ramekins. Cover with foil, crimping tightly around edge of baking pan. Bake in preheated oven for 30 minutes, or until pots de crème are set but still jiggly in the center. Remove pan from oven, remove foil, and take dish out of water bath and place on wire rack to cool to room temperature. Refrigerate until chilled, at least 4 hours or preferably overnight.

6. Meanwhile, prepare pralines (see page 311), substituting pine nuts for the pecans.

7. Place chilled ramekins on individual dessert plates. Spoon a large dollop of whipped cream on top of each ramekin. Sprinkle with coconut chips and add a piece of pine nut praline.

butterscotch panna cotta with chocolate espresso syrup

makes 6 servings

Panna cotta is a traditional cream-based Italian dessert. Much like ice cream, which has endless flavor variations, the cream in panna cotta can be infused with a variety of ingredients. Chai is quite popular at the moment, and I love the way the spices play off the smooth cream and the rich chocolate espresso sauce that I like to serve this with. If you're looking for a softer flavor, try infusing the cream with Earl Grey tea or even the classic vanilla bean. It doesn't matter what you go with, it's always good!

1 tbsp	gelatin	15 mL
2 tbsp	water	30 mL
3 tbsp	2% milk	45 mL
½ cup	packed dark brown sugar	125 mL
2¼ cups	heavy or whipping (35%) cream	560 mL
½	vanilla bean, split lengthwise	½
•	Chocolate Syrup (page 295)	•
1 tsp	espresso powder	5 mL

1. Lightly oil six ½-cup (125 mL) ramekins.
2. In a small bowl, dissolve gelatin in water. Set aside.
3. In a medium heavy-bottomed saucepan over medium heat, combine milk and brown sugar and cook, stirring constantly, until sugar dissolves. Stir in cream and vanilla bean and bring just to a boil. Remove pan from heat. Remove vanilla bean, slice in half lengthwise, and use the tip of a sharp knife to scrape the seeds back into the cream. Stir in prepared gelatin. Pour equal portions of mixture into prepared ramekins. Cover and refrigerate until chilled, for a minimum of 3 hours.
4. Meanwhile, prepare syrup, adding espresso powder while it is cooking.
5. Remove ramekins from refrigerator. To unmold, run a hot, wet knife between panna cotta and inside of ramekin. Invert ramekins onto individual serving plates and drizzle with chocolate espresso syrup.

tips

This recipe doubles or triples nicely.

This dessert can be made 1 to 2 days in advance and refrigerated until serving, but don't try freezing it (it will ruin the texture).

amaretti tiramisu

Every cook should have a good tiramisu recipe in their repertoire. This one uses amaretti, delicate almond-flavored Italian biscuits, instead of the traditional ladyfingers. For my taste, they give a bit more flavor and add a little something unexpected. You can make this in a large serving dish or dress it up in individual glasses as we have here. However you do it, just be sure that all the lovely layers are on display—it's half of what makes tiramisu so delightful!

½ cup	brewed espresso or strong coffee	125 mL
¼ cup	Marsala wine or brandy	60 mL
4	large free-range egg yolks	4
2 tbsp	granulated sugar	30 mL
2	large free-range egg whites	2
2 cups	mascarpone	500 mL
36	amaretti cookies	36
¼ cup	dark cocoa powder	60 mL
•	6 glass jars, parfait glasses, or wine glasses, for serving	•

tip

The way you build this dessert is determined by the serving vessel(s) you use. If you use one large bowl, just cover the bottom with half of the dipped cookies, followed by half of the mascarpone, the cocoa, and the remaining dipped amaretti, ending with the remaining mascarpone filling. If you use individual glasses or jars, fit in whatever number of amaretti works in one layer and alternate layers of fillings until you fill the glass. There is no wrong way. Just be sure the layers of mascarpone filling are at least 1 inch (2.5 cm) thick for best results.

1. In a shallow bowl, combine espresso and Marsala and set aside.
2. In a medium heatproof glass or metal bowl, combine egg yolks and sugar. Set over a saucepan of simmering water (make sure water does not touch bottom of bowl) and whisk constantly until mixture lightens in color and forms ribbons when whisk is lifted, about 3 to 5 minutes. Remove from heat and set aside to cool for 5 minutes.
3. Meanwhile, in a mixing bowl, using an electric mixer on medium-high speed, beat egg whites to stiff peaks. Set aside.
4. Fold mascarpone, ½ cup (125 mL) at a time, into cooled egg yolk mixture, combining well after each addition. Fold mascarpone-yolk mixture into the egg whites and combine well. Set aside.
5. ASSEMBLE: Allow 6 amaretti cookies per serving, arranged in 2 layers, in 6 tall, straight-sided serving glasses (see picture). Dip 6 cookies, one at a time, into espresso-Marsala mixture. Place 3 in the bottom of each serving glass. Fill each glass one-half full with mascarpone mixture and sprinkle with cocoa powder. Repeat with a layer of 3 cookies per glass, mascarpone and cocoa powder. Cover and refrigerate until served.

Choux Puffs with Salted Caramel
Ice Cream (page 232) and Chocolate
Ganache (page 307)

choux puffs with salted caramel ice cream and chocolate ganache

makes 1 dozen puffs

Choux puffs are, by their very nature, decadent. Now marry those rich pastry layers with salted caramel ice cream and chocolate ganache and your dinner guests will be beside themselves with delight. There is a definite technique to getting the dough right here, but it's not as hard as you may think. It just takes a lot of elbow grease and recognizing the silky shine that says the pastry is ready for piping. When piping these, it also helps to make a template by drawing little circles on one side of your parchment paper, flipping it over, and then piping into the outlines. This way, all of your choux will be consistent in size.

tip

See my YouTube video on how to make choux puffs.

1 cup	water	250 mL
½ cup	unsalted butter, cut into ½-inch (1 cm) cubes, softened	125 mL
2 tbsp	granulated sugar	30 mL
¼ tsp	fine sea salt	1 mL
1 cup + 2 tbsp	all-purpose flour	250 mL + 30 mL
4	large free-range eggs	4
1	egg, beaten	1
•	Salted Caramel Ice Cream (page 232)	•
•	Chocolate Ganache (page 307)	•

1. Preheat oven to 400°F (200°C). Line 2 baking sheets with parchment paper.
2. In a medium saucepan over medium heat, bring water, butter, sugar, and salt just to a boil and cook, stirring often, until butter is completely melted. Remove pan from heat and vigorously stir in flour (it will form a mass of dough). Put saucepan back on medium heat for a minute or so, stirring to boil off any excess water. Remove from heat and set aside to let cool for about a minute. Beat in eggs, one at a time, making sure to thoroughly combine each before adding the next. (Do not try adding all the eggs at once. The batter will be too difficult to mix and become a slippery mess.)

3. Using a pastry bag fitted with a medium-size tip or two spoons, mound dough, 1 tbsp (15 mL) at a time, on prepared baking sheets, spaced about 2 inches (5 cm) apart. Brush the top of each with egg wash. Bake in preheated oven for 10 minutes. Reduce the oven to 325°F (160°C) and bake for an additional 15 to 20 minutes, or until dry and golden. Remove pan from oven and set aside to cool for 2 to 3 minutes.

4. Slice each choux puff in half horizontally. If they are still soft in the center, place the halves cut-side up on the baking sheets and return to oven for 1 to 2 minutes to crisp up. Remove from oven and set aside to cool completely.

5. To serve, place bottom half of puffs on individual serving plates, fill each with a scoop of ice cream and a generous spoonful of ganache, and cover with top of puffs. Drizzle with ganache.

frozen
desserts

for best results

Ice cream is arguably the most popular dessert of all time. On its own in a bowl or on a cone, or drizzled with a decadent sauce and piled high with fruit, there's nothing else quite like it. Here I include not only recipes that require an ice-cream maker, but also semifreddos, which do not. I've also included a recipe for ice-cream sandwiches made with Raincoast Crisps. (Move over cupcakes, ice-cream sandwiches are the new it dessert!) Use your imagination when it comes to flavor and texture and play with the base recipes.

01 · The quantity of sugar in your ice cream will have a huge effect on the results, so don't be tempted to cut back. Too little sugar and you won't get the lovely creamy texture you desire. Too much sugar and the results will be sticky and cloying. Follow the recipe exactly.

02 · Allow as much time as possible for any flavorings to infuse the base recipe. For example, if you are using a vanilla bean or citrus peel, leave it in the base right up until you are pouring it into the ice-cream maker for the greatest flavor.

03 · If you have the space, store the bowl of the ice-cream maker in your freezer. It needs to be chilled for at least 8 hours ahead of time to get cold enough to give the best results.

04 · When making semifreddos, line your pan with enough plastic wrap or parchment paper so that you can fold it back onto itself once it is frozen. This makes for easy removal from the pan.

05 · If including alcohol in your recipe, be careful with the quantity. Too much alcohol will inhibit the dessert from freezing completely.

06 · When adding dried fruit, nuts, or chocolate, chop them finely so they don't interfere with the overall texture of the ice cream or semifreddo.

07 · Unlike store-bought varieties, homemade ice cream and semifreddo contain no preservatives and stabilizers, so keep them frozen right up until you are ready to serve because they will start melting right away. If you have time, chill your plates or serving bowls.

08 · For ease, use a hot, wet knife or scoop to serve your ice cream or semifreddo.

vanilla semifreddo

makes 12 servings

A semifreddo (which translated means "half cold") is a partially frozen Italian dessert that has the texture of frozen mousse and is slightly richer than ice cream. It can be poured into and served directly from molds, sliced from loaves, or even scooped onto cones. Unlike ice cream, however, it requires no custard making or churning. It comes together quickly and can be served within a few hours of making it. This recipe is for classic vanilla—always a hit—but as you'll see from the following pages, it's extremely versatile and can be flavored with almost anything, from fruit to nuts to chocolate to liquor.

4	large free-range eggs, separated	4
½ cup	granulated sugar, divided	125 mL
1 cup	heavy or whipping (35%) cream	250 mL
1½ tsp	pure vanilla extract	7 mL

1. Line a 9- by 5-inch (23 by 12.5 cm) loaf pan with plastic wrap or parchment paper.
2. In a mixing bowl, using an electric mixer on medium-high speed, beat yolks and ¼ cup (60 mL) sugar until light and fluffy. Set aside.
3. In another mixing bowl, beat cream until it holds soft peaks. Add vanilla and mix until combined. Refrigerate until ready to use.
4. In a third mixing bowl, beat egg whites until soft peaks form. Add remaining ¼ cup (60 mL) sugar and continue mixing until firm (but not dry) peaks form.
5. Fold whipped cream into yolk mixture, then fold in half of the egg whites and mix until well combined. Gently fold in remaining egg whites. Pour into prepared loaf pan and freeze for at least 4 hours or preferably overnight. Slice with a hot knife to serve.

variation

To make Cointreau Semifreddo, substitute 2½ tbsp (37 mL) Cointreau for the vanilla.

Vanilla Ice Cream (this page), Candied Ginger & Macadamia Nut Semifreddo (page 225), Cranberry and Caramelized White Chocolate Semifreddo (page 222), and Chocolate & Gosling's Rum Semifreddo (page 226)

cranberry and caramelized white-chocolate semifreddo

makes 12 servings

4	large free-range eggs, separated	4
½ cup	granulated sugar, divided	125 mL
1 cup	heavy or whipping (35%) cream	250 mL
½ cup	dried cranberries	125 mL
⅔ cup	Caramelized White-Chocolate Chunks (recipe follows) or chunks of white chocolate	150 mL

1. Line a 9- by 5-inch (23 by 12.5 cm) loaf pan with plastic wrap or parchment paper.
2. In a mixing bowl, using an electric mixer on medium-high speed, beat yolks and ¼ cup (60 mL) sugar until light and fluffy. Set aside.
3. In another mixing bowl, beat cream until it holds soft peaks. Refrigerate until ready to use.
4. In a third mixing bowl, beat egg whites until soft peaks form. Add remaining ¼ cup (60 mL) sugar continue mixing until firm (but not dry) peaks form.
5. Fold whipped cream into yolk mixture, then fold in cranberries and caramelized white-chocolate chunks. Fold in half of the egg whites and mix until well combined. Gently fold in remaining egg whites. Pour into prepared loaf pan and freeze for at least 4 hours or preferably overnight. Slice with a hot knife to serve.

tips

Be patient while the chocolate is roasting. It won't look like anything is happening for quite a while, then all of a sudden it will change color and get crumbly and dry. Even if it doesn't come back together afterward, it still tastes yummy and can be added to cookies, brownies, and hot chocolate, among other things.

Make sure all your equipment is completely dry before making this recipe, otherwise the chocolate will seize immediately.

caramelized white chocolate

makes about 1½ cups (375 mL)

| 1 lb | good-quality white chocolate (preferably Valrhona), chopped into small chunks | 500 g |
| • | Fine sea salt | • |

1. Preheat oven to 250°F (120°C). Spread chocolate in a single layer over a rimmed baking sheet. Roast in preheated oven for about 45 minutes, using a spatula to stir and spread chocolate around every 5 to 10 minutes (don't worry if it looks lumpy and crumbly at times—it will smooth out as you continue to stir), until chocolate turns a toffee color. Stir in sea salt to taste.

2. Spread roasted chocolate evenly over a baking sheet lined with parchment paper. Set aside to harden, about 60 minutes. Once completely hardened, break into ½-inch (1 cm) pieces. Transfer to an airtight container. Note that the cooled chocolate may look mottled, which is normal for untempered chocolate. Store at room temperature (it should keep for several months). (You can also pour the melted chocolate into an airtight jar, if desired—it will harden as it cools. To use, place it in a pot of barely simmering water.)

candied ginger and macadamia nut semifreddo

makes 12 servings

4	large free-range eggs, separated	4
½ cup	granulated sugar, divided	125 mL
1 cup	heavy or whipping (35%) cream	250 mL
¼ cup	candied ginger, chopped into small chunks	60 mL
½ cup	chopped toasted salted macadamia nuts	125 mL

1. Line a 9- by 5-inch (23 by 12.5 cm) loaf pan with plastic wrap or parchment paper.
2. In a mixing bowl, using an electric mixer on medium-high speed, beat yolks and ¼ cup (60 mL) sugar until light and fluffy. Set aside.
3. In another mixing bowl, beat cream until it holds soft peaks. Refrigerate until ready to use.
4. In a third mixing bowl, beat egg whites until soft peaks form. Add remaining ¼ cup (60 mL) sugar and continue mixing until firm (but not dry) peaks form.
5. Fold whipped cream into yolk mixture, then fold in ginger and nuts. Fold in half of the egg whites and mix until well combined. Gently fold in remaining egg whites. Pour into prepared loaf pan and freeze for at least 4 hours or preferably overnight. Slice with a hot knife to serve.

date and bourbon semifreddo

makes 12 servings

4	large free-range eggs, separated	4
½ cup	granulated sugar, divided	125 mL
1 cup	heavy or whipping (35%) cream	250 mL
2 ½ tbsp	bourbon	37 mL
½ cup	pitted Bahir or Medjool dates, coarsely chopped	125 mL

continued . . .

1. Line a 9- by 5-inch (23 by 12.5 cm) loaf pan with plastic wrap or parchment paper.
2. In a mixing bowl, using an electric mixer on medium-high speed, beat yolks and ¼ cup (60 mL) sugar until light and fluffy. Set aside.
3. In another mixing bowl, beat cream until it holds soft peaks. Add bourbon and mix until combined. Refrigerate until ready to use.
4. In a third mixing bowl, beat egg whites until soft peaks form. Add remaining ¼ cup (60 mL) sugar and continue mixing until firm (but not dry) peaks form.
5. Fold whipped cream into yolk mixture, then fold in dates. Fold in half of the egg whites and mix until well combined. Gently fold in remaining egg whites. Pour into prepared loaf pan and freeze for at least 4 hours or preferably overnight. Slice with a hot knife to serve.

chocolate and gosling's rum semifreddo

makes 12 servings

1 cup	heavy or whipping (35%) cream	250 mL
4 oz	70% bittersweet (dark) chocolate, finely chopped	125 g
4	large free-range eggs, separated	4
½ cup	granulated sugar, divided	125 mL
2½ tbsp	Gosling's Rum	37 mL

1. Line a 9- by 5-inch (23 by 12.5 cm) loaf pan with plastic wrap or parchment paper.
2. In a heavy-bottomed saucepan over low heat, heat cream just to a boil. Remove from heat and add chocolate. Set aside for 2 to 3 minutes to melt. Whisk until smooth. Refrigerate until completely cool.
3. In a mixing bowl, using an electric mixer on medium-high speed, beat yolks and ¼ cup (60 mL) sugar until light and fluffy. Set aside.
4. In another mixing bowl, beat cream until it holds soft peaks. Add bourbon and mix until combined. Refrigerate until ready to use.
5. In a third mixing bowl, beat egg whites until soft peaks form. Add remaining ¼ cup (60 mL) sugar and continue mixing until firm (but not dry) peaks form.
6. Fold whipped cream into yolk mixture, then fold in half of the egg whites and mix until well combined. Gently fold in remaining egg whites. Pour into prepared loaf pan and freeze for at least 4 hours or preferably overnight. Slice with a hot knife to serve.

vanilla ice cream

makes 1 quart (4 cups/1 L)

Making your own ice cream is easy with an ice-cream maker (the machines are readily available). Not only do you know exactly what is in your ice cream—avoiding the fillers and preservatives—but the flavor possibilities are innumerable. Here I provide the classic vanilla base and also give you a few of my favorite flavors (see pages 232 to 233). Once you get the hang of these, I encourage you to get creative and come up your own flavor combinations!

1 cup	whole milk	250 mL
2 cups	heavy or whipping (35%) cream	500 mL
½ tsp	pure vanilla extract	2.5 mL
½ cup	granulated sugar	125 mL
1	plump vanilla bean	1
6	large free-range egg yolks	6

1. In a medium heavy-bottomed saucepan, combine milk, cream, sugar, and vanilla.
2. Using a sharp knife, split the vanilla bean in half lengthwise and scrape the seeds from the pod into the cream, adding the pod. Stir to combine. Heat the mixture on medium heat, stirring constantly, until sugar has completely dissolved. Remove from heat.
3. In a mixing bowl, beat the eggs yolks until pale in color. Whisk a few tablespoons of hot cream mixture into the yolks, then whisk the yolk mixture back into the pan of cream. Heat on low heat, stirring constantly, until the custard thickens (when you draw your finger across the back of a spoon covered in it, your finger should leave a trail).
4. Pour through a fine-mesh sieve into a bowl; discard vanilla pod. Set aside to cool slightly, then cover and refrigerate for at least 3 hours, until thoroughly chilled. Follow the directions for your ice-cream maker.

frango

makes 1 quart (4 cups/1 L)

I'm so nostaligic about this recipe—my mother has made this luscious frozen dessert to serve at her dinner parties for years. It's nice on its own, but partnering it with light-as-air French Brandy Snaps with Almonds (page 256) or White-Chocolate Hazelnut Cookies (page 37) makes it suitable for even the most formal of tables.

1 cup	2% milk	250 mL
1 cup	packed golden brown sugar	250 mL
4	large free-range eggs, divided	4
2 cups	heavy or whipping (35%) cream	500 mL
½ tsp	flaked sea salt	2.5 mL

1. Line a 9- by 5-inch (23 by 12.5 cm) loaf pan with plastic wrap or parchment paper.
2. In a metal bowl, whisk together milk, sugar, and egg yolks. Set over a saucepan of simmering water (make sure water does not touch bottom of bowl). Cook, whisking constantly, until thickened slightly. Remove from heat and set aside to cool to room temperature.
3. Meanwhile, in a mixing bowl, using an electric mixer on medium-high speed, beat the cream until it holds soft peaks. Fold in cooled egg mixture.
4. In a separate mixing bowl, using an electric mixer on medium-high speed, beat egg whites until just stiff. Fold into cream mixture until just combined. Pour into prepared loaf pan. Cover and freeze for at least 4 hours or overnight. Slice with a hot knife to serve.

wildflower honey ice cream

makes 1 quart (4 cups/1 L)

1 cup	whole milk	250 mL
2 cups	heavy or whipping (35%) cream	500 mL
¾ cup	wildflower honey	175 mL
6	large free-range egg yolks	6

1. In a medium heavy-bottomed saucepan over medium heat, combine milk, cream, and honey, stirring constantly, until honey has completely dissolved. Remove from heat.
2. In a mixing bowl, by hand, beat the eggs yolks until well combined, about 2 minutes. Whisk a few tablespoons of hot cream mixture into the yolks, then whisk the yolk mixture back into the pan of cream. Heat on low heat, stirring constantly, until the custard thickens (when you draw your finger across the back of a spoon covered in it, your finger should leave a trail).
3. Pour through a fine-mesh sieve into a bowl. Set aside to cool slightly, then cover and refrigerate. Follow the directions for your ice-cream maker.

salted caramel ice cream

makes 1 quart (4 cups/1 L)

1 cup + ¾ cup	granulated sugar	250 mL + 175 mL
½ cup	water, divided	125 mL
1 cup	whole milk	250 mL
2 cups	heavy or whipping (35%) cream	500 mL
6	large free-range egg yolks	6

1. In a medium heavy-bottomed saucepan over medium-high heat, combine 1 cup (250 mL) granulated sugar and ¼ cup (60 mL) water. Bring to a boil and simmer until the sugar turns a rich golden color. Remove pan from the heat and add ¼ cup (60 mL) warm water. Return pan to medium heat and simmer until sugar has completely melted. Set aside.
2. In another medium heavy-bottomed saucepan over medium heat, combine milk, cream, and prepared caramel, stirring constantly until caramel has completely dissolved. Remove from heat.

3. In a mixing bowl, by hand, beat the eggs yolks until well combined, about 2 minutes. Whisk a few tablespoons of hot cream mixture into the yolks, then whisk the yolk mixture back into the pan of cream. Heat on low heat, stirring constantly, until the custard thickens (when you draw your finger across the back of a spoon covered in it, your finger should leave a trail).
4. Pour through a fine-mesh sieve into a bowl. Set aside to cool slightly, then cover and refrigerate. Follow the directions for your ice-cream maker. Add ¾ tsp (3 mL) flaked sea salt to the ice cream during the final stages of it turning in the ice-cream maker.

blood orange ice cream

makes 1 quart (4 cups/1 L)

3	blood oranges, divided	3
1 cup	whole milk	250 mL
2 cups	heavy or whipping (35%) cream	500 mL
¾ cup	granulated sugar	175 mL
6	large free-range egg yolks	6

1. Using a vegetable peeler, peel 1 blood orange (avoiding bitter pith as much as possible); reserve peel and orange.
2. In a medium heavy-bottomed saucepan over medium heat, combine orange peel, milk, cream, and sugar, stirring constantly until sugar has completely dissolved. Remove from heat.
3. In a mixing bowl, by hand, beat the eggs yolks until well combined, about 2 minutes. Whisk a few tablespoons of hot cream mixture into the yolks, then whisk the yolk mixture back into the pan of cream. Heat on low heat, stirring constantly, until the custard thickens (when you draw your finger across the back of a spoon covered in it, your finger should leave a trail).
4. Finely grate the zest from the remaining 2 oranges and add to the custard. Squeeze ½ cup (125 mL) juice from the oranges and add to the custard, stirring well.
5. Pour through a fine-mesh sieve into a bowl; discard peel. Set aside to cool slightly, then cover and refrigerate. Follow the directions for your ice-cream maker.

raincoast crisp ice-cream sandwiches

makes 6 sandwiches

I was sitting in the kitchen one day enjoying a small dish of ice cream. Sitting on the counter in front of me was a box of Raincoast Crisps. Without thinking too much about it, I broke off a corner of one of the crisps and dipped it into my bowl—it was love at first taste! I knew the crisps went well with just about everything, but who knew how good they would be as the backbone for this traditional childhood favorite? Below I present two flavor combinations, but you can make them in any combination that appeals to you. For a gluten-free option, make these with oat crisps—equally yummy and wheat-free!

cranberry hazelnut ice-cream sandwiches

12	Cranberry Hazelnut Raincoast Crisps	12
6	large scoops ice cream (flavor of your choice; see pages 220 to 239)	6
½ cup	toasted ground hazelnuts	125 mL

salty date and almond ice-cream sandwiches

12	Salty Date and Almond Raincoast Crisps	12
6	large scoops Salted Caramel Ice Cream (page 232)	6
½ cup	toasted flaked almonds (optional)	125 mL

1. Line a baking sheet with parchment paper. Place hazelnuts or almonds in a shallow dish.
2. Arrange 6 crisps on prepared baking sheet. Place a scoop of ice cream in the middle of each. Sandwich with a second crisp, gently pressing together to push the ice cream out to the edges.
3. Lightly press each side of the sandwich in the nuts or almonds, coating ice-cream edges completely (if using). Freeze in resealable bag until ready to serve.

frozen lemon cream with warm blueberries and lemon clove cookies

makes 8 servings

This is as fresh as it gets. When the days are hot and you're looking for a light, refreshing dessert, reach for this frozen cream.

tips

Use a hot knife to cut ice cream into slices.

The frozen lemon cream will keep for up to 2 weeks in an airtight container in the freezer.

lemon cream

2 cups	water	500 mL
¾ cup	granulated sugar	175 mL
1 tsp	coarsely grated lemon zest	5 mL
1½ tsp	unflavored gelatin, softened in 2 tbsp (30 mL) of cold water	7 mL
⅛ tsp	fine sea salt	0.5 mL
⅓ cup	freshly squeezed lemon juice	75 mL
•	Granulated sugar	•
1 cup	heavy or whipping (35%) cream	250 mL

warm blueberries

1½ cups	fresh blueberries	375 mL
1 tsp	finely grated lemon zest	5 mL
1 tbsp	freshly squeezed lemon juice	15 mL
1 tbsp	granulated sugar	15 mL
•	Lemon Clove Cookies (page 19)	•

1. Line an 8- by 4-inch (20 cm by 10 cm) loaf pan with plastic wrap.
2. MAKE LEMON CREAM: In a large saucepan, over medium heat, bring water, sugar, and lemon zest to a boil. Reduce heat and simmer for 10 minutes. Remove from heat and stir in softened gelatin. Stir in salt. Strain through double thickness of cheesecloth or a paper coffee filter into a bowl. Cover and refrigerate until cold but not set, about 15 minutes.
3. Remove from fridge. Stir in lemon juice. Pour into prepared loaf pan. Freeze until almost firm, then cover and freeze for at least 3 hours longer.
4. Remove from freezer. Turn mixture into the bowl of a food processor fitted with the metal blade and pulse until just slushy. Add cream and purée until smooth. Return to same loaf pan relined with clean plastic wrap. Freeze until firm, then cover and freeze for at least 3 hours longer or overnight.
5. MAKE BLUEBERRIES: In a large sauté pan over medium-high heat, while constantly shaking the pan, warm blueberries, lemon zest, lemon juice, and sugar until sugar is just dissolved and blueberries are glistening.
6. To serve, spoon warm blueberries next to a slice of Lemon Cream and decorate with 2 Lemon Clove Cookies.

life after death with cinnamon red wine sauce

makes 8 servings

Life After Death is the encore to my Death by Chocolate dessert, which was originally made for Bishop's Restaurant in Vancouver. The incredible combination of Marsala and white chocolate makes after-dinner ice-cream a sophisticated adult decadence.

6	large free-range egg yolks	6
2 tbsp	granulated sugar	30 mL
2 tbsp	Marsala wine	30 mL
1 cup	whole milk	250 mL
9 oz	white chocolate, finely chopped	275 g
2 cups	heavy or whipping (35%) cream, whipped to soft peaks	500 mL
•	Cinnamon Red Wine Sauce (page 299)	•

1. Line an 8-inch (20 cm) square metal baking pan with plastic wrap, leaving a generous overhang on all sides of the pan.
2. In a large bowl, whisk together egg yolks, sugar, and Marsala. Set aside.
3. In a heavy-bottomed saucepan over medium heat, warm milk until it just starts to bubble (but not boil). Remove from heat.
4. Whisking constantly, very slowly pour milk into egg yolk mixture. Pour mixture back into the saucepan and return to stovetop, on low heat. Using a wooden spoon, stir custard until it starts to thicken (when you draw your finger across the back of a spoon covered in it, your finger should leave a trail). Remove from heat and immediately stir in the white chocolate. Let sit for a few minutes to allow it to melt, then stir to combine. Set aside to cool to room temperature.
5. Fold whipped cream into the cooled custard. Pour into prepared baking pan. Freeze for at least 5 hours, or preferably overnight. Once the custard is frozen, fold the overhanging plastic wrap over it to prevent it from getting freezer burn.
6. To serve, scoop a ball of frozen custard onto individual dessert plates or bowls and drizzle with Cinnamon Red Wine Sauce.

variation

Pair with Salty Date and Almond Raincoast Crisps and make ice-cream sandwiches (page 235).

holiday favorites

for best results

Christmastime is the time for baking and desserts. Here I share some of my favorite holiday recipes, from traditional shortbread cookies to desserts that, as my son says, kick it up a notch: Christmas cake chock full not of candied fruit but of dried tart cherries, chocolate, and toasted pecans; Christmas trifle with raspberries, chocolate mousse, and chocolate sponge; and cheesecake with mincemeat. I hope these recipes make your holiday tables a bit more special and help to create some fond memories for you and your family.

01 · Holiday season is always stressful so let holiday baking be your de-stressor—either by enjoying the time in the kitchen creating something homemade or by taking the time to enjoy the delicious results.

02 · Christmas cakes are best when made a few weeks in advance so flavors have time to meld (be sure to wrap them well).

03 · Make several batches of shortbread and freeze the dough so you have something at the ready to bake for last-minute gatherings.

04 · The Chocolate Yule Log, which is a Christmas Eve tradition at our house, can be made and kept in the refrigerator for several days (the ganache keeps the cake moist) or you can freeze it for up to 1 month in advance (just make sure it is well wrapped). Either way, bring the cake to room temperature before serving.

05 · Semifreddos are great to have in the freezer at this time of year. You can simply slice off what you need and serve it with a sauce you already have on hand.

06 · Presentation is everything. Start looking for interesting jars, tins, trays, and baskets in which to package cookies, loaves, and candy well before the holidays. Visit your local nursery or even artist supply studios for packaging ideas.

07 · Many cookware, specialty food, and bakery shops sell attractive paper liners that you can bake cakes and loaves in and are brilliant for gift-giving. Keep an extra-long roll of heavy cellophane and a spoolful of pretty fabric ribbon handy.

mexican hot chocolate

makes 2½ cups (625 mL)

Homemade hot chocolate is the perfect winter treat. This version contains cinnamon, but try it with a shot of Peppermint Schnapps or Grand Marnier along with a dollop of whipped cream or a homemade marshmallow. It's oh-so-decadent.

1 cup	dark cocoa powder (preferably Valrhona or Bendorf)	250 mL
1½ cups	granulated sugar	375 mL
1 tsp	ground cayenne pepper	5 mL
½ tsp	ground cinnamon	2.5 mL
¾ cup	2% milk (or richer if you prefer)	175 mL

1. In a medium bowl, combine cocoa powder, sugar, cayenne pepper, and cinnamon. Store in an airtight container.
2. In a small saucepan, combine 2 tbsp (30 mL) of the cocoa mixture and 1 tbsp (15 mL) milk to make a paste. Gradually (to avoid lumps) whisk in remaining milk. Set over medium heat and stir gently until the milk just starts to boil. Remove from heat and serve immediately, topped with a dollop of whipped cream or a marshmallow, if desired.

chai tea blend

makes about 1⅓ cups (325 mL)

I was first introduced to chai at Vij's Restaurant in Vancouver where, because of their no-reservation policy, everyone (even the likes of Jamie Lee Curtis and Anthony Bourdain) lines up for dinner. This is my personal spice blend, which has a warmth and heat that makes a great base for many desserts or just a wonderful drink all on its own.

2 oz	loose-leaf black tea (not perfumed)	60 g
2 tsp	cardamon pods	10 mL
2 tsp	cinnamon sticks, broken into ½-inch (1 cm) pieces	10 mL

In a bowl, combine tea, cardamom, and cinnamon. Store in an airtight container.

chai tea for two

1 cup	2% or whole milk	250 mL
1 cup	water	250 mL
2 tbsp	granulated sugar	30 mL
2 tbsp	Chai Tea Blend (recipe above)	30 mL

1. In a medium saucepan, combine milk, water, and sugar and bring to a boil. Stir in chai tea blend. Cover pan, remove from heat, and set aside for 2 minutes to steep.
2. Using a fine-mesh sieve, strain into 2 serving cups or mugs (discard solids). Serve immediately, adding more sugar if you prefer it sweeter.

granny's sugar cookies

makes 3 to 4 dozen cookies (depending on cookie cutter)

Of all the sugar cookies I've eaten in my life, I think these are by far my favorite. Not too sweet, with a clean, crisp snap, they are almost foolproof to make. (Just be sure not to bake them too long; you don't want them brown around the edges.) Kids love cutting these out and decorating them. To make rolling a bit easier and to avoid having to add too much extra flour, roll the dough out on a piece of parchment paper the size of your baking sheet, cut out the cookies, then simply pull the excess dough away. Voila! Your cookies are ready to pop in the oven—no transfer, no mess.

3 cups	all-purpose flour	750 mL
1 cup	granulated sugar	250 mL
½ tsp	baking powder	2.5 mL
½ tsp	fine sea salt	2.5 mL
1 cup	cold unsalted butter, cut into ½-inch (1 cm) cubes	250 mL
1	cold large free-range egg	1
3 tbsp	cold heavy or whipping (35%) cream	45 mL
1 tsp	pure vanilla extract	5 mL

1. In a large bowl, sift together flour, sugar, baking powder, and salt. Add butter cubes and stir to coat with flour. Using a pastry cutter, cut butter into small, pea-sized pieces. Working quickly, blend with your fingers until mixture is the consistency of coarse sand. (You may do this in a food processor, but you will have to do it in 2 batches.)

2. In a separate small bowl, whisk together egg, cream, and vanilla. Quickly stir into flour mixture until well combined. Remove dough from the bowl and, using your hands, form into a ball, gently kneading together if necessary. Press into a flat disk, wrap in plastic wrap, and refrigerate until chilled, at least 1 hour.

3. Preheat oven to 325°F (160°C). Line 2 baking sheets with parchment paper.

4. Remove chilled dough from refrigerator. Divide dough into 2 equal portions. On a lightly floured surface, roll out 1 portion to ¼-inch (0.5 cm) thickness. Cut out desired shapes with a cookie cutter or an inverted glass lightly dipped in flour. Place shapes on prepared cookie sheet. Repeat with second portion of dough. Bake in preheated oven for 8 to 10 minutes, or until edges show just a hint of golden brown. Remove from oven and cool on baking sheets for 2 to 3 minutes before turning out onto a wire rack to cool completely.

tip

You can brush the top of the unbaked cookies with some cream and sprinkle them with coarse white sugar or make fondant to decorate them once they are baked.

cranberry florentines

makes 4 dozen cookies

Nutty, lacy, and wafer-thin, Florentines are a Christmas classic. This version uses dried fruit instead of candied fruit and adds a kick of ginger. A real treat.

½ cup	salted butter	125 mL
½ cup	packed golden brown sugar	125 mL
2 tbsp	corn syrup	30 mL
½ cup	all-purpose flour	125 mL
½ cup	dried cranberries	125 mL
⅓ cup	candied ginger, slivered	75 mL
½ cup	flaked almonds	125 mL
½ cup	slivered almonds	125 mL

tips

If you find the mixture is spreading too much when baking, return to the stove and simmer for another minute or two. If the mixture is too thick, add 1 tbsp (15 mL) heavy or whipping (35%) cream.

If you like, drizzle Florentines with melted dark chocolate after they have cooled.

1. Preheat oven to 325°F (160°C). Line 2 baking sheets with parchment paper.
2. In a large heavy-bottomed saucepan over medium-high heat, combine butter, sugar, and corn syrup. Bring to a boil, reduce heat, and simmer, whisking constantly, for about 2 minutes, until the sugar is completely dissolved. Remove from the heat. Add flour, cranberries, ginger, and almonds and stir until well combined.
3. Using a teaspoon, drop mounds of dough on prepared baking sheets, spaced about 3 inches (7.5 cm) apart. Bake in preheated oven for 10 to 12 minutes, or until slightly darker around the edges. Remove from oven and cool on baking sheets for 5 minutes before turning out onto a wire rack to cool completely.

shortbread cookies

makes 2 dozen cookies

Shortbread always makes an appearance at Christmastime, but don't just relegate these simple and reliable cookies to your holiday lineup. Make them all year long! They go with fresh fruit, sorbets and ice creams, and even a strong blue cheese and glass of port.

2 cups	unsalted butter, softened	500 mL
1 cup	granulated sugar	250 mL
4 cups	all-purpose flour	1 L
½ cup	additional all-purpose flour, for kneading	125 mL
•	Superfine sugar	•

1. Preheat oven to 275°F (140°C). Line 2 baking sheets with parchment paper.
2. In a mixing bowl, using an electric mixer on medium-high speed, cream butter and sugar until light and fluffy. Add flour 1 cup (250 mL) at a time, mixing well after each addition.
3. Dust pastry board with flour for kneading. Turn dough out onto prepared pastry board and knead until smooth. Roll out to 1-inch (2.5 cm) thickness. Cut out 2-inch (5 cm) circles using a cookie cutter or an inverted glass lightly dipped in flour or cut 4- by 1-inch (10 by 2.5 cm) rectangles using a sharp knife. Transfer shapes to prepared baking sheets. Bake in preheated oven for 30 to 40 minutes, watching carefully toward the end of the baking time (remove from oven before color changes). Dust with superfine sugar. Cool on baking sheets for 2 to 3 minutes before transferring to a wire rack to cool completely.

tip

Superfine sugar, also known as berry sugar, is often used as a finishing sugar and to make meringues. You can make your own by whizzing granulated sugar in a food processor fitted with the metal blade for a couple of minutes. You will end up with a little less volume, so if you need a specific amount, add a bit more and measure after processing.

dried cherry almond shortbread cookies

makes 3 dozen cookies

There are never enough varieties of shortbread in my house once the holidays roll around. As soon as the kids smell them baking, there's a lineup in the kitchen waiting for them to cool! These make lovely gifts for family and friends.

1 cup	unsalted butter, softened	250 mL
1 cup	lightly packed light brown sugar	250 r
2 cups	all-purpose flour, sifted	
½ cup	dried cherries	
½ cup	slivered blanched almonds	

1. Preheat oven to 350°F (180°C). Line 2 baking shee
2. In a medium mixing bowl, using an electric mi
   cream butter and sugar until light and fluf
   Stir in cherries and almonds. Turn ou
   using your hands, form a disk. Divide di
   into a log (round or squared off) about 2½ i
   plastic wrap and refrigerate for at least 1 hour.
3. Using a sharp knife, slice dough crosswise into ¼
   squares. Arrange on prepared baking sheets, spaced
   in preheated oven for 10 to 15 minutes, or until firm an   cool
   completely on baking sheets. Store in an airtight containe.   reeze
   for up to 1 month.

variations

01 · You can substitute dried blueberries or finely chopped apricots or cranberries for the dried cherries.

02 · Instead of dried fruit, try making these with ¼ cup (60 mL) cocoa nibs.

Dried Cherry Shortbread Cookies (this page)
and *Cranberry Rugelach* (page 265)

praline shortbread cookies

makes 3½ dozen cookies

These shortbreads are buttery, nutty, and chewy—and with their shimmering pecan centers, they look as though they've been adorned with jewels.

2 cups	unsalted butter, softened	500 mL
1 cup	granulated sugar	250 mL
4 cups	all-purpose flour	1 L
•	Pecan Praline (recipe follows)	•

1. In a large mixing bowl, using an electric mixer on medium-high speed, cream butter and sugar until light and fluffy. Gradually add flour and mix until well combined. Scrape dough onto a clean, lightly floured work surface. Divide dough into 2 equal portions. Roll each portion into a log about 2 inches (5 cm) in diameter. Wrap both logs in plastic wrap and refrigerate for at least 1 hour.
2. Preheat oven to 250°F (120°C). Line 2 baking sheets with parchment paper.
3. Using a sharp knife, cut dough into slices ⅛ inch (3 mm) thick. Transfer slices to prepared baking sheet. Press a praline pecan into the center of each cookie. Bake in preheated oven for 12 to 15 minutes, until just golden around the edges.

pecan praline

makes 1 cup (250 mL)

1 cup	granulated sugar	250 mL
½ cup	water	125 mL
1 cup	pecan halves	250 mL

1. Grease a 13- by 9-inch (33 by 23 cm) baking sheet with vegetable oil.
2. In a medium heavy-bottomed saucepan over medium heat, combine sugar and water. Bring to a boil and cook until mixture turns an amber color, removing the pan from the heat occasionally and swirling pan to even out the coloring. Do not stir. Once the mixture is deep golden, add pecans, swirling pan to coat pecans well. Pour mixture evenly over prepared baking sheet, using a spatula to spread mixture out to edges. Set aside to cool completely.
3. Using your hands, break praline into small pieces, ensuring a pecan is included in each piece.

pecan chocolate shortbread cookies

makes 4 dozen cookies

This is by far my favorite shortbread. It has all the components of a great cookie: melt-in-your mouth gooey chocolate, a crisp butter crumb, and a nutty pecan crunch. I recommend making large batches of these—they are definitely a treat to be shared with family and friends.

3½ cups	all-purpose flour	875 mL
⅛ tsp	fine sea salt	0.5 mL
2 cups	unsalted butter, softened	500 mL
1 cup	confectioners' (icing) sugar	250 mL
¾ cup	pecans, toasted and coarsely chopped	175 mL
8 oz	Valrhona chocolate, chopped into small chunks	250 g

1. In a large bowl, sift together flour and salt. Set aside.
2. In a mixing bowl, using an electric mixer on medium-high speed, cream butter and sugar until light and fluffy. Gradually mix in dry ingredients until just combined. Add pecans and chocolate and mix until well combined. Cover and refrigerate until chilled, at least 2 hours.
3. Preheat oven to 325°F (160°C). Line 2 baking sheets with parchment paper.
4. Remove dough from refrigerator. Using a small ice-cream scoop, drop balls of dough on prepared baking sheets, spaced about 1¼ inches (3 cm) apart. Press down slightly. Bake in preheated oven for 8 to 10 minutes, or until barely brown. Remove from oven and cool on baking sheets for 5 minutes before transferring to a wire rack to cool completely.

french brandy snaps with almonds

makes about 20 flat cookies or cigars · makes about 10 tulip cups

These were one of the first "fancy" cookies I ever made, and in university they became my go-to dinner party dessert. Shaped into cigars or tulip cups, they can be made ahead and then filled (think fruit and cream, lemon curd, orange-scented whipped cream, flavored marscapone, mousse, Bailey's, or Grand Marnier crema . . .) just before serving. Elegant and very versatile.

½ cup	all-purpose flour	125 mL
1 tsp	ground ginger	5 mL
¼ tsp	fine sea salt	1 mL
½ cup	unsalted butter	125 mL
½ cup	packed golden brown sugar	125 mL
½ cup	corn syrup	125 mL
1 tsp	freshly squeezed lemon juice	5 mL
½ tsp	pure vanilla extract	2.5 mL
½ cup	flaked almonds, lightly toasted	125 mL

1. Preheat oven to 375°F (190°C). Line 2 baking sheets with parchment paper.
2. In a medium bowl, combine flour, ginger, and salt. Set aside.
3. In a medium saucepan over low heat, melt butter with brown sugar, corn syrup, lemon juice, and vanilla and bring just to a boil. Remove from the heat. Gradually whisk in the dry ingredients until well combined. Stir in almonds.
4. Drop dough, 1 tsp (5 mL) at a time, on prepared baking sheets, spaced about 3 inches (7.5 cm) apart. Bake in preheated oven for 6 to 8 minutes, or until edges are golden.
5. FOR FLAT COOKIES: Remove from oven and cool on baking sheets for 5 minutes before turning out onto a wire rack to cool completely.
6. FOR CIGARS: Remove from oven and cool on baking sheets for 1 minute. Roll a cookie around the handle of a wooden spoon, let it set briefly, carefully slide it off the handle, and place on a wire rack to cool completely. Repeat with remaining cookies.
7. FOR TULIP CUPS: Remove from oven and cool on baking sheets for 1 minute. Drape cookies over upside-down teacups or ramekins and set aside to cool completely.

French Brandy Snaps with Almonds
(this page), Cranberry Florentines
(page 248), and Noël Snowballs (page 264)

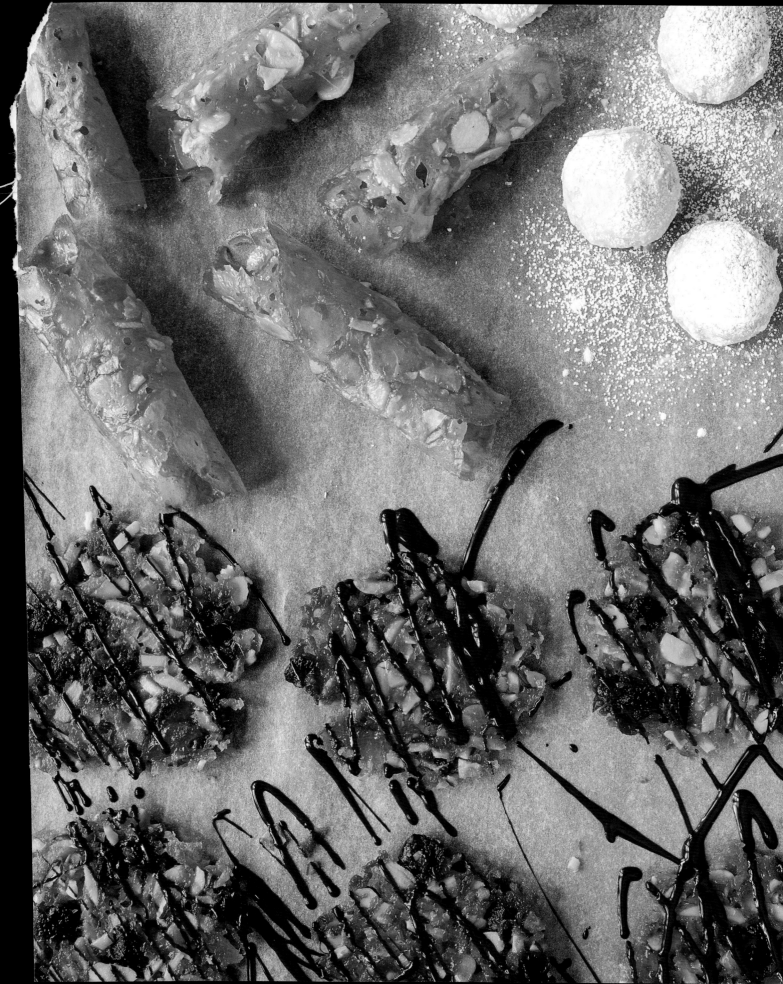

holleo cookies

makes 2 dozen cookie sandwiches

This is my take on a cookie sandwich and, according to hundreds of customers at our store, they are infinitely more yummy. Always a favorite during the holidays, we had a hard time keeping them in stock. Kids love the chocolately leaf-shaped cookies and creamy filling while adults love the subtle depth of the dark cocoa and sophisticated delicacy of the marscapone. These can be made in advance, but are best assembled on the day they are to be eaten, as the filling will soften the cookie if they sit for a long time.

cookies

1½ cups	all-purpose flour	375 mL
½ cup	unsweetened cocoa powder	125 mL
⅛ tsp	fine sea salt	0.5 mL
Pinch	ground cinnamon	Pinch
1 cup	cold unsalted butter	250 mL
½ cup	granulated sugar	125 mL

filling

½ cup	heavy or whipping (35%) cream	125 mL
¾ cup	mascarpone	175 mL
2 tsp	granulated sugar	10 mL
½ tsp	Cointreau or brandy	2.5 mL
•	Confectioners' (icing) sugar or unsweetened cocoa powder	•

1. MAKE COOKIES: In a large bowl, sift together flour, cocoa, salt, and cinnamon. Set aside.
2. In a mixing bowl, using an electric mixer on medium-high speed, cream cold butter and sugar until light and fluffy. Add dry ingredients and mix until just combined. Using your hands, form dough into a ball and flatten, then cover in plastic wrap and freezer for 1 hour.
3. Line 2 baking sheets with parchment paper. Remove dough from freezer. Roll out to ¼-inch (0.5 cm) thickness. Cut into holly shapes using a cookie cutter and place on prepared baking sheets, spaced about 1 inch (2.5 cm) apart. Cover and refrigerate for at least 1 hour.
4. Preheat oven to 200°F (100°C).

5. Remove chilled cookies from refrigerator. Bake in preheated oven for 35 to 45 minutes, or until dry and firm. Remove pan from oven and set aside until cooled completely.

6. MAKE FILLING: Place the mascarpone in a small bowl. Set aside.

7. In a mixing bowl, using an electric mixer on high speed, beat the cream until soft peaks form. Fold into the mascarpone, along with the sugar and Cointreau. (This filling can be made ahead and be kept in the refrigerator for several hours before using.)

8. ASSEMBLE: Take one cookie and spread a scant 1 tbsp (15 mL) of filling onto the bottom. Place the flat side of a second cookie onto the filling to form a sandwich. Repeat with remaining cookies and filling. Dust the top of each cookie sandwich with confectioners' sugar or cocoa. Refrigerate until serving. (These cookies need to be filled and eaten the same day. Can be made up to 4 hours in advance of serving.)

tips

These are also yummy filled with Chocolate Ganache (page 307). For a bit of extra holiday cheer, crush a couple of candy canes and stir them into the ganache or mascarpone filling.

Java Sticks (page 262), *Chocolate Mint Crackle Cookies* (page 263), and *Holleo Cookies* (page 258)

java sticks

makes 6 dozen cookies

When I was young I could always tell Christmas was just around the corner when I saw my mother making Java Sticks. She would stand there dipping each end in chocolate, telling us kids that we'd be in "deep yogurt" if we snuck any out of the tins—"for company only!" I still always managed to get a few, and to this day they are one of my favorite holiday treats.

1 cup	unsalted butter, softened	250 mL
½ cup	superfine sugar	125 mL
2 tsp	finely ground espresso	10 mL
1½ cups	all-purpose flour, sifted	
¼ cup	ground pecans	60 mL
3 oz	70% bittersweet (dark) chocolate, finely chopped	90 g
1 cup	finely chopped pecans	250 mL

1. Preheat oven to 350°F (180°C). Line 2 baking sheets with parchment paper.
2. In a medium mixing bowl, using an electric mixer on medium-high speed, cream butter and sugar until light and fluffy. Add coffee, flour, and nuts and mix until combined.
3. Transfer dough to a piping bag fitted with a #6 tip. Pipe dough onto prepared baking sheets in 3-inch (7.5 cm) lengths spaced about 1¼ inch (3 cm) apart. Bake in preheated oven for 10 to 15 minutes or until edges are golden. Remove from oven and cool on baking sheets for 5 minutes before transferring to a wire rack to cool completely.
4. In a small bowl set over a saucepan of simmering water (make sure water does not touch bottom of bowl), melt chocolate, stirring until smooth. Dip one end of each cookie in chocolate and transfer to a wire rack with parchment or wax paper underneath. Sprinkle ends with pecans and set aside until chocolate is set, about 10 minutes.

tips

You can skip dipping the ends of the cookies in chocolate, but I think it makes them rather special.

By all means, sprinkle the Java Sticks with whatever nuts you prefer—just be sure they are finely chopped.

chocolate mint crackle cookies

makes 3 dozen cookies

These are a great addition to your holiday cookie stash and the perfect gift for chocolate mint fans. I love the delicate chocolate cracks in the otherwise snowy shell—so pretty and perfect for the Christmas season.

12 oz	70% bittersweet (dark) chocolate	375 g
4 oz	unsalted butter	125 g
2	large free-range eggs	2
2 tbsp	granulated sugar	30 mL
2 tsp	pure mint extract	10 mL
½ cup	Simple Sugar Syrup (page 294)	125 mL
1 cup	all-purpose flour	250 mL
1 tbsp	baking powder	15 mL
½ tsp	fine sea salt	2.5 mL
1 cup	confectioners' (icing) sugar	250 mL
1 cup	granulated sugar	250 mL

1. In a heavy-bottomed saucepan over low heat, melt chocolate, butter, and vanilla.
2. In a medium bowl, whisk together eggs and sugar until thickened and light yellow in color. Whisk in simple sugar syrup and mint extract. Set aside.
3. In a separate bowl, sift together flour, baking powder, and salt. Set aside.
4. To the chocolate mixture, slowly add egg and sugar mixture, whisking continuously until well combined. Add flour mixture and stir well (the mixture will be very loose). Cover and refrigerate for at least 3 hours or overnight.
5. Preheat oven to 350°F (180°C). Line 2 baking sheets with parchment paper. Place confectioners' sugar in small shallow dish.
6. Shape dough, a scant 1 tbsp (15 mL) at a time, into even balls, rolling in granulated sugar and then coating each in confectioners' sugar before placing on prepared baking sheets, spaced 3 inches (7.5 cm) apart. Bake in preheated oven for 10 to 12 minutes, until cookies are just set in the middle (be careful not to overcook). Remove from oven and cool on baking sheets for 3 to 5 minutes before turning out onto a wire rack to cool completely.

tip

To achieve a nice crackle effect, be very generous when rolling the dough balls in the sugars.

noël snowballs

makes 3 dozen cookies

A twist on traditional Mexican wedding cake cookies, these snowballs make a delightful addition to any holiday dessert platter. They're the perfect one-bite sweet for cocktail parties or a quiet moment with a cup of chai (page 245).

2¼ cups	all-purpose flour	550 mL
½ cup	confectioners' (icing) sugar	125 mL
¼ tsp	fine sea salt	1 mL
1 cup	unsalted butter, softened	250 mL
2 tbsp	liquid honey	30 mL
1 tsp	finely grated orange zest	5 mL
¾ cup	finely chopped pecans	175 mL
•	Confectioners' (icing) sugar	•

tip
. . . .

You can experiment with these: try changing the nuts and substituting lemon or lime zest for the orange zest.

1. In a large bowl, sift together flour, sugar, and salt. Set aside.
2. In a mixing bowl, using an electric mixer on medium-high speed, cream butter and honey until fluffy. Add dry ingredients and mix until just combined. Stir in orange juice and pecans until well combined. Wrap dough in plastic wrap and refrigerate until chilled, at least 2 hours.
3. Remove from fridge. Shape dough, 2 tsp (10 mL) at a time, into even balls (about the size of cherry tomatoes) and place on prepared baking sheets, spaced at least 1 inch (2.5 cm) apart. Refrigerate until chilled, about 30 minutes.
4. Preheat oven to 350°F (180°C) and line 2 baking sheets with parchment paper.
5. Bake in preheated over for 10 to 12 minutes, or until firm. Remove from oven and cool on baking sheets for about 2 minutes (the cookies should still be warm) before rolling in confectioners' sugar and transferring to a wire rack to cool completely.

cranberry rugelach

makes 2 dozen rugelach

Cranberries and spices and crisp, layered pastry—this is the first recipe I reach for in November when I begin my seasonal baking. I have to admit, they are so irresistible that I have a hard time stopping myself from eating them all fresh out of the oven. And their aroma when baking is the best holiday scent there is.

1½ cups	dried cranberries	375 mL
1 cup	dried currants	250 mL
1 tbsp	ground allspice	15 mL
2 tsp	ground cinnamon	10 mL
½ tsp	ground cloves	2.5 mL
¼ cup	packed golden brown sugar	60 mL
¼ cup	granulated sugar	60 mL
2 tbsp	salted butter, melted	30 mL
•	Cream Cheese Pastry (page 318)	•
1	large free-range egg, beaten	1
•	Coarse (sanding) sugar	•

1. Preheat oven to 350°F (180°C). Line a baking sheet with parchment paper.
2. In a large bowl, combine cranberries, currants, allspice, cinnamon, cloves, brown and granulated sugars, and butter.
3. Roll cream cheese dough into a 12- by 9-inch (30 by 23 cm) rectangle. Sprinkle filling evenly over the dough. Using a sharp knife, cut the dough lengthwise into three 12- by 3-inch (30 by 7.5 cm) strips. Then cut widthwise across the strips to make twelve 4- by 3-inch (10 by 7.5 cm) rectangles. Cut diagonally across each rectangle to create 2 triangles. Starting at the wide end, roll up each triangle, making sure filling doesn't fall out. Transfer to prepared baking sheet. Brush tops with beaten egg and sprinkle with coarse sugar. Bake in preheated oven for 15 to 20 minutes, or until golden. Remove from oven and cool on baking sheet for 3 to 5 minutes before turning out onto a wire rack to cool completely.

tips

This cookie is one of my holiday favorites; however, they are best eaten the day they are made. You can freeze the cooled baked rugelach in resealable bags and warm them up in a 325°F (160°C) oven for a couple of minutes to get that just-baked texture.

You can find coarse sugar in the baking section of most good grocery stores. If you can't get your hands on any, use demerara sugar.

The filling for this cookie will keep for several weeks in an airtight container in the refrigerator and is a fantastic topping for muffins.

mincemeat cheesecake

makes one 9-inch (23 cm) cheesecake

My mother made this cheesecake every year at Christmas. It takes the well-known and loved flavors of mincemeat and marries them with a dense and delicious New York–style cheesecake—delicious! It's perfect for a dessert buffet, as it can be made in advance, freezes well, and slices beautifully.

	crust	
½ cup	unsalted butter, melted	125 mL
2 cups	graham cracker crumbs or shortbread cookie crumbs	500 mL

	middle layer	
1¾ cups	mincemeat, preferably homemade or good-quality store-bought	425 mL

	top layer	
16 oz	cream cheese (not whipped)	500 g
⅓ cup + 2 tbsp	orange juice	75 mL + 30 mL
4 cups	marshmallows	1 L
1 cup	heavy or whipping (35%) cream, whipped to soft peaks	250 mL

1. Preheat oven to 350°F (180°C).
2. MAKE CRUST: In a medium saucepan over low heat, melt butter. Stir in graham cracker crumbs. Pour into a 9-inch (23 cm) springform pan. Press firmly and evenly into the bottom of the pan. Bake in preheated oven for 10 minutes, or until golden around the edges. Remove from oven and cool completely in the pan.
3. Spread the mincemeat filling on top of cooled crust.
4. MAKE TOPPING: In the top of a double-boiler, over simmering water, melt marshmallows with ⅓ cup (75 mL) orange juice, stirring to combine. Remove from heat and set aside to cool.
5. In a mixing bowl, using an electric mixer on medium-high speed, cream together cream cheese and 2 tbsp (30 mL) orange juice until well combined. Add cooled marshmallow mixture. Fold in whipped cream.
6. Pour topping over mincemeat filling. Cover and refrigerate until chilled, at least 3 hours or overnight.
7. Serve with softly whipped cream on the side or pipe rosettes along the top edge of the cake.

tips

This cheesecake will keep in an airtight container in the freezer for up to 1 month.

Use a hot, wet knife to cut clean slices.

pumpkin gingersnap cheesecake

makes one 9-inch (23 cm) cheesecake

Not everyone loves pie with their holiday turkey, so if you're looking for alternatives, try this cheesecake. It has all the classic requirements: a rich and creamy pumpkin filling and a warming spiced gingersnap crust. My stepson Douglas insists upon this when he's home for the holidays, so it's now part of our family tradition.

crust

1½ cups	gingersnap crumbs	375 mL
½ cup	unsalted butter, melted	125 mL
2 tbsp	granulated sugar	30 mL

filling

2 cups	cream cheese, softened	500 mL
1 cup	sour cream	250 mL
½ cup	lightly packed light brown sugar	125 mL
2 tbsp	cornstarch	30 mL
4	large free-range eggs	4
1 cup	pure pumpkin purée	250 mL
2 tsp	pure vanilla extract	10 mL
1 tsp	ground ginger	5 mL
½ tsp	ground cinnamon	2.5 mL
Large pinch	ground nutmeg	Large pinch
Large pinch	ground allspice	Large pinch
Pinch	ground cloves	Pinch

1. MAKE CRUST: Preheat oven to 350°F (180°C).
2. In a mixing bowl, combine gingersnap crumbs, butter, and sugar. Press evenly into the bottom and partially up the sides of a 9-inch (23 cm) springform pan. Bake in preheated oven for 10 minutes, until firm and slightly golden. Remove from oven and set aside.
3. MAKE FILLING: Reduce oven temperature to 325°F (160°C).
4. In a mixing bowl, using an electric mixer on medium-high speed, beat cream cheese until smooth. Add sour cream, sugar, and cornstarch and mix until combined. Add eggs and mix until combined. Add pumpkin purée, vanilla, and all the spices and mix until just combined (be careful not to overmix).

continued . . .

5. Pour mixture into prepared crust.

6. On the lowest oven rack, place a shallow pan of water (this will keep the air in the oven moist and help prevent the cheesecake from cracking). Place cheesecake on middle oven rack and bake in preheated oven for 1¼ hours. Turn oven off, open oven door slightly (prop open with oven mitt, if necessary), and let sit for 15 minutes. Remove from oven and set aside to cool in the pan. After about 10 minutes, loosen the sides of the cheesecake with a sharp knife (this also helps to prevent cracking). Once cheesecake has cooled to room temperature, refrigerate.

7. ASSEMBLE: Serve chilled garnished with Hazelnut Praline (page 311) and a bowl of whipped cream alongside so guests can serve themselves.

tip

When the internal temperature of a cheesecake goes above 160°F (71°C) while baking, it will often crack. To help prevent this, turn the oven off when the cheesecake reaches 150°F (70°C) in the center (use an instant-read thermometer to test for doneness). Shock from a sudden change in temperature can also cause cracking, which is why letting the cheesecake rest for a while before you remove it from the oven is a good idea.

chocolate raspberry trifle

makes 12 to 16 servings

Every Christmas our family anticipated my Great-Aunt Morci's trifle (she was a fabulous cook and baker). It was layered with sponge, custard, fruit, cream, and "a lot of work," my mother used to say, and we were always extremely happy that Aunt Morci would volunteer to bring it. In honor of my aunt (and to satisfy my chocolate cravings), I came up with this version of trifle. A number of this dessert's components can be made ahead so making it doesn't seem so daunting, and the whole thing must be assembled at least a day ahead so the flavors marry. It serves a lot of people, so go for it! You won't regret the accolades, and you may just start a new tradition of your own.

custard

¾ cup	granulated sugar	175 mL
⅔ cup	sifted cornstarch	150 mL
½ tsp	fine sea salt	2.5 mL
3 cups	scalded milk	750 mL
3	large free-range eggs, beaten	3
1 tbsp	butter	15 mL
2 tsp	pure vanilla extract	10 mL

chocolate mousse

2 cups	heavy or whipping (35%) cream	500 mL
16 oz	70% bittersweet (dark) chocolate, finely chopped	500 g
¼ cup	Grand Marnier	60 mL
Large pinch	fine sea salt	Large pinch
8	large free-range eggs, separated	8

raspberry sauce

20 oz	thawed frozen raspberries	567 g
½ cup	raspberry preserves	125 mL
2 tbsp	granulated sugar	30 mL
¼ cup	Kirsch	60 mL

chocolate sponge

1 cup	granulated sugar	250 mL
1 cup	all-purpose flour	250 mL
½ tsp	baking soda	2.5 mL
½ cup	safflower oil	125 mL

continued . . .

tip

To scald milk, heat milk in a saucepan over medium heat just until bubbles form around the edge of the pan (do not boil).

2 tsp	pure vanilla extract	10 mL
1 cup	cold orange juice	250 mL
2 tbsp	white vinegar	30 mL
·	Chocolate shavings or curls	·
·	Cocoa powder	·

1. MAKE CUSTARD: In a large heatproof bowl, whisk together sugar, cornstarch, salt, and milk. Place over a saucepan of simmering water (do not let water touch bottom of bowl) and heat, stirring occasionally, for 10 to 15 minutes, until mixture thickens slightly. Set aside.

2. In a medium mixing bowl, whisk together ½ cup (125 mL) custard mixture and eggs. Add mixture to pan with remaining custard and cook for another 5 minutes, stirring until thickened. Remove pan from heat and stir in butter and vanilla. Set aside to cool to room temperature, then cover with plastic wrap and refrigerate.

3. MAKE MOUSSE: In a medium heavy-bottomed saucepan over medium heat, bring cream just to a boil. Remove pan from heat and add the chocolate. Set aside for 2 to 3 minutes, until chocolate has melted. Whisk in Grand Marnier and salt, until smooth. Set aside to cool slightly, then, one at a time, add egg yolks.

4. In a mixing bowl, using an electric mixer on medium-high speed, beat egg whites until stiff (but not dry). Working in two batches, fold into chocolate mixture. Set aside in refrigerator to chill.

5. MAKE SAUCE: In a medium saucepan over medium heat, combine raspberries, preserves, and sugar and cook for 5 minutes, until mixture coats the back of a spoon. Set pan aside to cool. Stir in Kirsch.

6. MAKE SPONGE: In a mixing bowl, combine sugar, flour, and baking soda.

7. Preheat oven to 350°F (180°C). Butter a 9-inch (23 cm) springform pan and line bottom with parchment paper.

8. In a small bowl, combine oil, vanilla, and orange juice. Add to dry ingredients and stir until combined. Stir in vinegar and quickly pour into prepared pan. Bake in preheated oven for 30 minutes, until the sponge is dry and bounces back when lightly touched. Remove pan from oven and set aside to cool completely. Release cake from pan and, using a sharp knife, slice crosswise in 3 equal pieces to form 3 even sponge layers.

9. ASSEMBLE: Line a large straight-sided glass bowl with 1 layer of sponge. Spread one-third of raspberry sauce over top, and then spoon over custard. Place another sponge layer on top and cover with another one-third of the raspberry sauce. Cover with half of the chocolate mousse. Place last sponge layer on top and spread with remaining raspberry sauce. Top with the remaining chocolate mousse. Refrigerate until ready to serve. Garnish with chocolate shavings or curls and dust with cocoa.

cranberry currant crumble tart

makes one 9-inch (23 cm) tart

I think anything with a good crumble topping is worth indulging in—especially if it's served warm with ice cream on a cold, wet, or snowy night. This is a great tart to enjoy over the holiday season when you're wanting something easy but comforting. Serve with vanilla or cinnamon ice cream.

	Press pastry for one 9-inch (23 cm) shell (page 317)	

filling

½ cup	dried currants	125 mL
½ cup	granulated sugar	125 mL
3 tbsp	pure maple syrup	45 mL
½ tsp	pure vanilla extract	2.5 mL
1 tbsp	brandy	15 mL
•	Zest of 1 lemon	•
2 cups	fresh or frozen cranberries	500 mL

crumble topping

2¾ cups	all-purpose flour	675 mL
1½ cups	packed golden brown sugar	375 mL
2 tsp	ground cinnamon	10 mL
1 tsp	pure vanilla extract	5 mL
¾ cup	cold unsalted butter, cut into ½-inch (1 cm) cubes	175 mL
8 oz	almond paste, cut into ½-inch (1 cm) pieces (page 319)	250 g

1. Preheat oven to 350°F (180°C). Line a 9-inch (23 cm) shallow, fluted tart pan with press pastry, pressing dough up the sides to extend ⅛ inch (3 mm) above rim of the pan. Bake in preheated oven for 15 to 20 minutes, until top edge of pastry is slightly pale golden. Remove from oven and set aside to cool slightly.
2. MAKE FILLING: In a medium bowl, combine currants, sugar, maple syrup, vanilla, brandy, and lemon zest. Add cranberries and mix to coat. Spoon into baked pastry shell.
3. MAKE TOPPING: In a large bowl, combine flour, sugar, and cinnamon. Sprinkle with vanilla. Add butter and almond paste and rub into the flour mixture until evenly combined (it's okay if the mixture is a bit clumpy). Spread over the filling, completely covering the cranberries.
4. Bake in preheated oven for 40 to 50 minutes, or until the filling is bubbling and the topping is golden brown. Remove from oven and place on a wire rack to cool.

chocolate tart with winterfruit compote

makes one 9-inch (23 cm) tart

This sings of the holiday season: the smell of the dried fruit, red wine, and cinnamon simmering on the stove is fabulous. It's also a good go-to recipe when you need a dessert for a crowd in a hurry. It's quite rich, will easily serve 10, and you can make the filling well in advance. If you really want to gild the lily, serve it with Crème Anglaise (see page 303)—delicious.

·	Press pastry for one 9-inch (23 cm) shell (page 317)	·
1 cup	Chocolate Ganache (page 307)	250 mL
2 cups	Spiced Winterfruit Compote (page 309)	500 mL

1. Preheat oven to 350°F (180°C).
2. Line a 9-inch (23 cm) shallow, fluted tart pan with press pastry, pressing dough up the sides to extend ⅛ inch (3 mm) above rim of the pan. Bake in preheated oven for 15 to 20 minutes, until top edge of pastry is slightly pale golden. Remove from oven and set aside to cool slightly.
3. Spread bottom of baked, cooled pastry shell with ganache.
4. Spoon compote evenly over ganache. Serve at room temperature.

chocolate chestnut torte

makes one 9-inch (23 cm) torte

The subtle but distinctive flavor of chestnut marries beautifully with chocolate. Elegant, rich, but not cloying, this single-layer cake is perfect for a seasonal dinner party.

torte

5 oz	70% bittersweet (dark) chocolate, chopped	150 g
½ cup	unsalted butter	125 mL
8 oz	unsweetened chestnut purée	250 g
6	large free-range eggs, at room temperature, separated	6
¾ cup	granulated sugar	175 mL
¾ cup	ground almonds	175 mL

glaze

½ cup	heavy or whipping (35%) cream	125 mL
8 oz	70% bittersweet (dark) chocolate, finely chopped	250 g
8	halves candied chestnuts	8

tip
....

I often will fold some sweetened chestnut purée into the whipped cream. Simply combine ⅓ cup (75 mL) chestnut purée and 1 cup (250 mL) heavy or whipping (35%) cream. This doubles the enjoyment, as chestnut is a fairly subtle flavor.

1. MAKE TORTE: Preheat oven to 350°F (180°C). Butter a 9-inch (23 cm) springform pan.
2. In a medium heavy-bottomed saucepan on lowest setting, melt chocolate and butter together, stirring occasionally. Remove from the heat and stir in chestnut purée until well combined. Set aside to cool.
3. In a mixing bowl, using an electric mixer on medium-high speed, beat egg yolks and sugar together until pale and foamy.
4. In another bowl, beat egg whites to soft peaks.
5. Fold chocolate mixture into egg yolk mixture. Fold in almonds, and then fold in prepared egg whites. Pour into prepared springform pan. Bake for 35 to 40 minutes, until dry on top but still moist in the center. Remove from oven and set aside to cool completely.
6. MAKE GLAZE: In a small heavy-bottomed saucepan, bring cream to a boil. Remove from the heat and stir in the chocolate. Set aside for 2 to 3 minutes, until chocolate has melted. Whisk until smooth. Set aside for 2 to 3 minutes more to thicken.
7. ASSEMBLE: Remove sponge from the pan. Trim the top to create an even surface. Place cake on a cooling rack with a piece of parchment paper underneath. Pour prepared glaze over the cake. Using a spatula, spread glaze over the sides to cover. Carefully transfer cake to a serving platter. Decorate around the top edge of the cake with candied chestnuts. Serve with a bowl of softly whipped cream to pass around.

cranberry upside-down cake

makes one 9-inch (23 cm) cake

Is there anything more seasonal than the ruby-red gleam of cranberries? They make this cake so pretty, and I love the contrast of the tart cranberries and the sweet butter caramel sponge.

topping

¼ cup	unsalted butter, softened	60 mL
¼ cup	granulated sugar	60 mL
6 tbsp	packed golden brown sugar	90 mL
1 bag (12 oz)	fresh cranberries	1 bag (375 g)

cake

¼ cup	unsalted butter, softened	60 mL
½ cup	packed golden brown sugar	125 mL
•	Finely grated zest of 1 lemon	•
•	Finely grated zest of 1 orange	•
2	large free-range eggs	2
½ cup	2% milk	125 mL
1 tsp	pure vanilla extract	5 mL
1¼ cups	all-purpose flour	300 mL
1½ tsp	baking powder	7 mL
½ tsp	fine sea salt	2.5 mL
½ bag (6 oz)	fresh cranberries	½ bag (175 g)
½ cup	chopped pecans, toasted	125 mL

tips

Lining the bottom of the pan with parchment paper is crucial; otherwise the cranberries will stick to the pan even if it is well buttered.

Be sure to fold the cranberries into the batter by hand—a mixer would mash the berries.

1. Preheat oven to 325°F (160°C). Line a 9-inch (23 cm) round cake pan with parchment paper. Butter and flour the sides and bottom.

2. MAKE TOPPING: In a small bowl, cream together butter and sugars. Spread on the bottom of prepared cake pan. Pour cranberries over butter mixture and press in.

3. MAKE CAKE: In a mixing bowl, using an electric mixer fitted with the paddle, on medium-high speed, cream the butter, sugar, and zests until light and fluffy. Add eggs one at a time, mixing and scraping down the sides of the work bowl after each addition. Add milk and vanilla and mix (it'll look like the batter is separating, but just carry on). Add flour, baking powder, and salt and mix until almost combined. By hand, fold in cranberries and pecans. Gently spread the batter over the cranberries in the cake pan. Bake in preheated oven for 45 to 60 minutes, or until the center springs back and cranberries are bubbling up around the sides. Remove from oven and cool in pan for 10 minutes. Run a knife around the outside of the cake. Place a platter face down over the pan. Holding both firmly, invert the pan to release the cake onto the platter. Remove the parchment, slice, and serve warm.

chocolate praline yule log

makes 14 to 16 servings

Yule logs began as a holiday tradition in France, usually with a white sponge cake, chocolate filling, and a buttercream finish. This version is chocolate overload, with a dark, moist sponge rolled around a praline ganache and covered in more ganache! Without fail, this is the dessert we always enjoy on Christmas Eve. You can make it as small or as large as your crowd demands. Make it really festive by garnishing with holly or evergreen branches, dusting with confectioners' sugar, and scattering with cranberries. Make this for your family and friends and you're sure to become a celebrity overnight.

	sponge	
9	large free-range eggs, at room temperature, separated	9
1¾ cups	granulated sugar, divided	425 mL
2¼ tbsp	all-purpose flour	33 mL
1 cup	dark cocoa powder (preferably Valrhona or Bendorf)	250 mL
3½ tbsp	unsalted butter, melted	50 mL

	ganache	
1½ lbs	70% bittersweet (dark) chocolate	750 g
3 cups	heavy or whipping (35%) cream	750 mL
¼ cup	Grand Marnier, Cointreau, Kahlua, or bourbon (optional)	60 mL
2 cups	Halzelnut Praline, roughly chopped (page 311, use half of this recipe)	500 mL

•	Confectioners' (icing) sugar	•
•	Holly sprigs	•
•	Evergreen sprigs and pinecones	•

1. MAKE SPONGE: Preheat oven to 350°F (180°C). Line 2 baking sheets with parchment paper.
2. In a mixing bowl, using an electric mixer on medium-high speed, beat egg yolks and half of the sugar until light and fluffy. Set aside.
3. In another mixing bowl, beat egg whites until soft peaks form. Mixing constantly, slowly add remaining sugar and beat until egg whites become stiff (but not dry) peaks.

continued . . .

4. Meanwhile, sift together cocoa and flour. Gently fold into egg yolk mixture. Fold in butter. Stir in two large spoonfuls of egg whites until just combined, then gently fold in remaining egg whites. Divide mixture in half and spread over the prepared baking sheets to a thickness of about ½-inch (1 cm). Bake in preheated oven for about 20 minutes or until a toothpick inserted into the middle comes out clean and sponge springs back lightly to the touch. Remove from oven and set aside to cool in pans.

5. MAKE GANACHE: In a small saucepan over medium heat, warm cream and butter just to boiling point. Remove from heat, add chocolate, then set aside for 3 to 4 minutes, until melted. Stir until smooth, then set aside to cool completely.

6. ASSEMBLE: Spread top of each sponge with a ¼-inch (0.5 cm) thick layer of ganache. Divide praline into 2 equal portions, then sprinkle evenly over each sponge.

7. Starting from the wide edge, carefully roll up sponge, peeling parchment off sponge as you go. Repeat with remaining sponge. Refrigerate for 4 to 6 hours to before trimming and assembling log. Use a sharp knife to trim the ends on a 20-degree angle, reserving the pieces.

8. Cut remaining sponge into 3 even pieces, again cutting on a 20-degree angle. Transfer largest rolled sponge to a large serving platter and arrange seam-side down. Arrange remaining 3 pieces beside and on top of it so they resemble branches.

9. Using a knife or metal spatula, spread remaining ganache evenly over sponges, making rough waves so ganache resembles bark. Make a swirl pattern on the ends to resemble the core of a log. Dust with confectioners' sugar. Garnish platter with holly and pieces of evergreen and pinecones.

dark-chocolate fruitcake

makes 10 mini fruitcakes or three 9- by 5-inch (23 by 12.5 cm) fruitcakes

Fruitcake has gotten a bad rap over the years and "regifting" jokes abound. Well, this cake is so good you'll be hoarding it for yourself! Deep dark chocolate, velvety port, nuts, and dried (not candied) fruit elevate this cake to the status of "I hope I am on the list for one of those dark-chocolate fruitcakes again this year!"

11 cups	mixed dried fruit (figs, cherries, and apricots cut in half; blueberries; cranberries)	2.75 L
2 cups	port, divided	500 mL
21 oz	70% bittersweet (dark) chocolate	630 g
1¾ cups	salted butter, softened	425 mL
1½ cups	granulated sugar	375 mL
11	large free-range eggs	11
1¾ cups	all-purpose flour	425 mL
1½ tsp	baking powder	7 mL
8 oz	bittersweet chocolate chips	250 g
7 cups	pecans and hazelnuts, toasted	1.75 L
1 cup	Simple Sugar Syrup (page 294)	250 mL

1. In a large bowl, combine fruit and 1 cup (250 mL) port, cover, and set aside to soak overnight at room temperature.
2. Preheat oven to 300°F (150°C). Line 10 mini loaf pans (5¾ by 3¼ inch/14.5 by 8 cm) or 3 loaf pans (9 by 5 inch/23 by 12.5 cm) with two crisscrossing pieces of parchment paper (each strip overlapping in opposite direction).
3. In a large bowl, sift together flour and baking powder. Set aside.
4. Melt chocolate in a medium heatproof glass or metal bowl set over a saucepan of simmering water (make sure water does not touch bottom of bowl), stirring often. Remove from heat and set aside.
5. In a mixing bowl, using an electric mixer on medium-high speed, cream butter and sugar until light and fluffy. Gradually mix in melted chocolate. Add eggs and mix well. Add dry ingredients and mix until just combined. Stir in chocolate chips. Stir in soaked fruit and nuts and combine well. Pour into prepared pans. Bake in preheated oven for 45 minutes to 1 hour for the mini pans or 1½ to 2 hours for regular loaf pans, or until a toothpick inserted into the center of cake comes out clean. Remove from oven and set aside to cool completely. Lifting the overhanging edges of the parchment, remove cake from pan. Peel away parchment.
6. In a small saucepan over medium heat, bring simple syrup and remaining 1 cup (250 mL) port just before boiling. Brush mixture heavily over baked cakes. Set cakes aside for 20 minutes, then brush warm mixture over cakes again. Allow cakes to cool completely (see Tips).

tips

To highlight the flavor of the port syrup, wrap the cakes in cheesecloth and soak the cheesecloth in the port syrup. Wrap tightly in plastic wrap and refrigerate. After 3 to 4 days, soak the cheesecloth in more port syrup.

You can wrap the finished cakes in plastic wrap and then foil until ready to serve or gift. If you prefer, decorate the tops of the cakes in marzipan.

These cakes are ready to enjoy the next day or can be frozen for up to 6 months.

toppings
& special
touches

for best results

The recipes in this chapter will elevate your good desserts to great desserts, and deliver the reactions you deserve without a lot more work on your part. I consider some of the recipes here absolute essentials: caramel sauce, raspberry coulis, crème fraîche, and ganache are always in my fridge. If you master only one thing, make it caramel sauce (go slowly the first time you make it and don't be distracted). Served warm or cold, sauces, coulis, and syrups not only enhance the flavor of a dessert, but also the texture and visual appeal. Do not be tempted to make shortcuts here.

01 · Make double the amount of sauce or coulis you need and refrigerate or freeze the extra. Label it so it doesn't get lost in the fridge or freezer.

02 · For each of the basic sauces, I have provided a number of variations. Use your imagination and experiment with ingredients. Just be careful not to add too much liquid—you want your sauces to have some viscosity.

03 · Use the best ingredients you can afford for the best results.

04 · Always strain your berry coulis (there's nothing worse than, say, a mouthful of blackberry seeds).

05 · Serve your desserts on dinner plates. Crowding dessert on a small plate never looks good and leaves little room to add your finishing touches.

06 · Buy some squeeze bottles from a cookware store and use these to add garnishes to your plates. They are much easier to control than a spoon.

07 · You will get compliments if you make a good dessert and present it with care. (Everyone remembers the starter and the dessert. The middle . . . not so much.)

simple sugar syrup

makes 1⅓ cups (325 mL)

1 cup	granulated sugar	250 mL
1 cup	water	250 mL

In a medium saucepan over medium heat, boil sugar and water, stirring occasionally, until sugar completely dissolves. Remove pan from heat and set aside to cool completely. Will keep for several months in an airtight container in the refrigerator.

variations

01 · **COFFEE SYRUP:** Replace water with an equal amount of brewed coffee.

02 · **TEA SYRUP:** Replace water with an equal amount of steeped tea.

03 · **LEMON GRASS SYRUP:** Smash a 2-inch (5 cm) piece of peeled lemongrass. Add to pan with water and sugar and leave in during storage. Strain syrup through a fine-mesh sieve before using.

04 · **CHOCOLATE SYRUP:** Combine 1 cup (250 mL) good-quality unsweetened cocoa powder (preferably Valrhona or Bensdorp) and ½ tsp (2.5 mL) fine sea salt with the sugar before adding the water. Whisk to combine. Bring to a boil and simmer for 2 to 3 minutes, until thickened slightly. Remove from heat and whisk in 1 tsp (5 mL) pure vanilla extract.

05 · **LEMON OR ORANGE SYRUP:** Peel 2-inch (5 cm) thick strips of lemon or orange peel from half a lemon or orange. Add to pan with water and sugar. Discard peel after syrup has cooled completely. If making lemon syrup, stir in 1 tbsp (15 mL) fresh lemon juice. If making orange syrup, stir in 1 tbsp (15 mL) Cointreau or Grand Marnier.

06 · **MOJITO SYRUP:** After removing simple syrup from heat, stir in ½ cup (125 mL) fresh mint leaves, 2 tbsp (30 mL) dark rum, and 1 tbsp (15 mL) fresh lime juice. Set pan aside until syrup is completely cooled, then strain through a fine-mesh sieve.

raspberry coulis

makes 1¼ cups (300 mL)

1¼ cup	frozen raspberries, thawed	300 mL
½ cup	confectioners' (icing) sugar	125 mL
1 to 2 tsp	freshly squeezed lemon juice	5 to 10 mL

In a food processor fitted with the metal blade, purée raspberries. Strain through a fine-mesh sieve into a mixing bowl, pressing with the back of a spoon to extract all the juice. Discard pulp. Stir in confectioners' sugar and lemon juice, to taste. Cover and refrigerate until ready to use. Will keep in airtight container in the refrigerator for up to 5 days and in the freezer for up to 3 months.

cranberry coulis

makes 1¼ cups (300 mL)

1 cup	cranberries, fresh or frozen	250 mL
1 cup	granulated sugar	250 mL
¼ cup	water	60 mL

In a medium saucepan over medium heat, cook cranberries, sugar, and water until sugar dissolves and cranberries begin to burst. Remove pan from heat and set aside to cool. Use as is or, for a smooth sauce, use the back of a wooden spoon to push the mixture through a food mill. Will keep in an airtight container in the refrigerator for up to 1 week or in the freezer for up to 1 month.

cinnamon red wine sauce

makes about 2 cups (500 mL)

1½ tsp	arrowroot	7 mL
1 tbsp	water	15 mL
1¾ cups	red wine	425 mL
½ cup	granulated sugar	125 mL
1	3-inch (7.5 cm) cinnamon stick	1

In medium saucepan over medium heat, combine arrowroot and water. Stir in wine. Bring to a boil, reduce heat, and simmer until mixture thickens slightly. Strain through a fine-mesh sieve into a bowl. Serve warm or cold. Will keep in an airtight container in the refrigerator for up to 1 month.

lemon curd

makes 1 cup (250 mL)

4	large free-range egg yolks	4
½ cup	granulated sugar	125 mL
¼ cup	finely grated lemon zest	60 mL
⅓ cup	freshly squeezed lemon juice	75 mL
⅛ tsp	fine sea salt	0.5 mL
6 tbsp	butter, cut into 6 pieces, softened	90 mL

1. In a large heatproof glass or metal bowl, whisk together egg yolks, sugar, lemon zest, lemon juice, and salt. Set over a saucepan of simmering water (make sure water does not touch bottom of bowl) and whisk constantly until yolks thicken and ribbons form when whisk is lifted from the bowl, 6 to 8 minutes. Remove bowl from heat. Whisk in butter 1 piece at a time.

2. Strain curd through a fine-mesh sieve into a bowl (discard solids). Set aside until cool. Spoon curd into a resealable jar. Refrigerate until ready to use. Will keep in an airtight container in the refrigerator for up to 1 week.

crème fraîche

makes 3 cups (750 mL)

3 cups	heavy or whipping (35%) cream (not ultra-pasteurized)	750 mL
3 tbsp	buttermilk or yogurt	45 mL

In a glass or porcelain bowl, combine cream and buttermilk. Cover loosely with plastic wrap and place in a warm spot away from drafts. Let stand for 24 to 48 hours, until thick (it should be the consistency of sour cream or yogurt). Refrigerate in an airtight container for up to 10 days.

Crème Anglaise: vanilla, chocolate, cinnamon, lemon (page 303)

crème anglaise

makes 2 cups (500 mL)

5	large free-range egg yolks	5
½ cup	granulated sugar	125 mL
Pinch	fine sea salt	Pinch
1 cup	2% milk	250 mL
½ cup	heavy or whipping (35%) cream	125 mL
½ tsp	pure vanilla extract or 1-inch (2.5 cm) piece vanilla bean, split in half	2.5 mL

1. In a stainless steel bowl, whisk together egg yolks, sugar, and salt until creamy. Set aside.
2. In a heavy-bottomed saucepan over medium-high heat, combine milk, cream, and vanilla and heat just until bubbles form around the edge (do not boil). Slowly whisk hot milk into yolk mixture.
3. Set bowl over a saucepan of simmering water (make sure water does not touch bottom of bowl) and, stirring constantly with a wooden spoon, cook until custard begins to thicken, about 4 or 5 minutes (it should be thick enough to coat the back of the spoon). Remove bowl from heat and immediately strain custard through a fine-mesh sieve into a clean bowl. Fill another bowl with ice and place the custard bowl overtop the ice to cool. Once cooled completely, transfer to an airtight container and refrigerate until ready to use. Will keep for up to 3 days in the refrigerator.

tip

See my YouTube video on how to make crème anglaise.

variations

01 · MAPLE CRÈME: Reduce sugar to ¼ cup (60 mL) and add 2 tbsp (30 mL) maple syrup and a pinch of nutmeg to the pan in step 1.

02 · ESPRESSO CRÈME: Add 3 tbsp (45 mL) finely ground espresso to pan in step 2 before heating.

03 · CHOCOLATE CRÈME: In step 3, after hot custard is removed from heat, whisk in ½ cup (125 mL) chopped bittersweet chocolate until melted, and then strain custard.

04 · CINNAMON CRÈME: Add ½ tsp (2.5 mL) ground cinnamon and one 3-inch (7.5 mL) stick of cinnamon to pan in step 2 before heating.

05 · ORANGE GRAND MARNIER CRÈME: Add three 1-inch (2.5 cm) strips of orange peel to pan in step 2 before heating. In step 3, whisk 1 tbsp (15 mL) Grand Marnier into the cooled sauce.

06 · BOURBON CRÈME: Substitute 1 tbsp (15 mL) bourbon for the vanilla.

tips

....

The key to a great caramel is allowing
the sugar syrup to cook, without
stirring, until it turns that rich amber
color. If you stop too early, it won't
have that lovely rich flavor. But watch
it carefully—it can burn quickly!

....

See my YouTube video on how
to make caramel sauce.

caramel sauce

makes 2 cups (500 mL)

1½ cups	granulated sugar	375 mL
½ cup	water	125 mL
1 cup	heavy or whipping (35%) cream, at room temperature	250 mL

1. In a large heavy-bottomed saucepan over low heat, combine sugar and water. Cook until sugar dissolves. Increase heat to medium-high. For more even caramelizing, swirl the mixture in the pan several times (do not use a spoon at this stage; the mixture can seize up and crystalize). Cook until mixture is a rich amber color. Remove pan from heat.
2. Slowly pour in cream (be careful, as the mixture will bubble up). Return to low heat and stir until smooth. Remove from heat and cool in pan. Store cooled caramel in airtight container in the refrigerator for up to 10 days or in the freezer for up to 3 months.

variations

01 · ORANGE CARAMEL SAUCE: Replace half the water with orange juice. At the end of step 2, before cooling, stir in finely grated zest from half an orange.

02 · ESPRESSO CARAMEL SAUCE: After step 1, before adding cream, add ¼ cup (60 mL) room temperature brewed espresso. It will bubble up, but stir to combine. Continue with step 2.

03 · MANGO CARAMEL SAUCE: At the end of step 2, before cooling, slowly stir in 1 cup (250 mL) room temperature mango juice. Be careful, as mixture will bubble up. Return to heat and stir until smooth. Remove from heat and continue with step 2.

04 · CHOCOLATE CARAMEL SAUCE: After adding cream and returning pan to low heat in step 2, add 2 oz (60 g) finely chopped bittersweet chocolate. Stir to combine and then continue with step 2.

butterscotch sauce

makes 2 cups (500 mL)

½ cup	packed golden brown sugar	125 mL
2 tbsp	unsalted butter	15 mL
1 tsp	pure vanilla extract	5 mL
2 tbsp	brandy	30 mL
½ cup	heavy or whipping (35%) cream	125 mL

In a small saucepan over low heat, combine sugar, butter, and vanilla and brandy and cook, stirring occasionally, until sugar dissolves completely. Stir in cream and simmer for 3 to 5 minutes, until thickened. Store in an airtight container in the refrigerator for up to 2 weeks or freeze for up to 2 months.

chocolate ganache

For glazes
makes 1½ cups (375 mL)

1 cup	heavy or whipping (35%) cream	250 mL
4 oz	70% bittersweet (dark) chocolate, finely chopped	125 g

For fillings
makes 1¾ cups (425 mL)

1 cup	heavy or whipping (35%) cream	250 mL
8 oz	70% bittersweet (dark) chocolate, finely chopped	250 g
1 tbsp	unsalted butter	15 mL

For truffles
makes 1¼ cups (300 mL)

½ cup	heavy or whipping (35%) cream	125 mL
8 oz	70% bittersweet (dark) chocolate, finely chopped	250 g
2 tbsp	unsalted butter	30 mL

In a heavy-bottomed saucepan, over medium-low heat, bring cream to a boil. Remove from heat and add chocolate. Let stand for 2 to 3 minutes, until chocolate melts. Add butter, if using. Stir until smooth. Cool in pan. If not using within a couple of hours, cover and refrigerate. Ganache will keep in an airtight container in the refrigerator for up to 2 weeks or in the freezer for up to 2 months. When ready to use, very gently reheat to desired consistency.

tip
See my YouTube video on how to make ganache.

chocolate hazelnut spread

makes one 8-ounce (250 g) jar

1 cup	hazelnuts, peeled and toasted	250 mL
½ cup	powdered sugar	125 mL
¼ cup	high-quality unsweetened dark cocoa powder	60 mL
¾ tsp	pure vanilla extract	3 mL
¼ tsp	kosher salt	1 mL
2 tbsp	grapeseed oil	30 mL

tip

....

This recipe doubles well.

In a food processor fitted with the metal blade, process hazelnuts until a smooth butter forms, about 3 minutes. Add sugar, cocoa powder, vanilla, salt, and grapeseed oil and continue processing until smooth and creamy. Spoon into a sterilized airtight jar and refrigerate. Will keep in the refrigerator for up to 2 weeks.

spiced winterfruit compote

makes 8 to 9 cups (2 to 2.25 L)

8	whole cloves	8
12	whole peppercorns	12
2	3-inch (7.5 cm) cinnamon sticks	2
•	Peel from ½ lemon, cut into wide strips	•
•	Peel from ½ orange, cut into wide strips	•
8	whole cardamom pods	8
2 cups	dried figs, halved	500 mL
2 cups	prunes	500 mL
2 cups	red wine	500 mL
½ cup	granulated sugar	125 mL
2 cups	dried apricots, halved if large	500 mL
2 cups	golden raisins	500 mL
2 cups	water	500 mL
½ cup	granulated sugar	125 mL

1. Place cloves, peppercorns, cinnamon, lemon and orange peel, and cardamom in a piece of cheesecloth. Bring up corners of cloth and tie securely with kitchen string.
2. In a large saucepan over low heat, combine figs, prunes, wine, and sugar. Add spice bag and simmer for 30 minutes. Remove from heat and set aside to cool completely. Drain excess liquid and reserve for another use.
3. In a separate saucepan over low heat, combine apricots, raisins, water, and sugar and simmer for 30 minutes. Remove from heat and set aside to cool completely. Drain excess liquid and reserve for another use.
4. Remove spice bag from figs and prunes and discard. Combine the 2 fruit mixtures and stir well. Place in an airtight container and refrigerate until ready to use. Will keep in an airtight container in the refrigerator for at least 1 month.

tips

The strained cooking liquid is flavorful. Mix a spoonful in a glass of sparkling water or wine. Or mix with some dried cherries or cranberries to make a quick sauce for ice cream.

hazelnut praline

makes 3 cups (750 mL)

1 cup	unsalted butter	250 mL
1 cup	granulated sugar	250 mL
3 tbsp	corn syrup	45 mL
⅓ cup	heavy or whipping (35%) cream	75 mL
2¼ cups	hazelnuts	560 mL

1. Preheat oven to 350°F (180°C). Line 2 baking sheets with parchment paper.
2. In a medium heavy-bottomed saucepan over medium-high heat, combine butter, sugar, corn syrup, and cream. Bring to a boil and cook for 1 minute. Stir in nuts. Reduce heat to medium and simmer for 3 minutes, until mixture turns light brown. Pour even amounts of the praline onto each baking sheet. Bake in preheated oven for 10 minutes, until golden brown. Remove from oven and set aside to cool completely.
3. Using your hands, break the praline into small chunks. Alternately, using a food processor fitted with the metal blade, grind praline until it reaches desired texture (you'll need to do this in 2 batches). Store in an airtight container at room temperature for up to 1 week or freeze for up to 2 months.

tip

See my YouTube video on how to make praline.

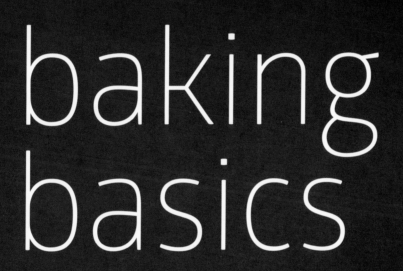

baking basics

for best results

This chapter includes the pastry recipes that are referenced in other parts of the book as well as a recipe for making your own almond paste. Once you discover how easy these basics can be to make, I know you'll soon begin creating your own dessert recipes. The press pastry is just as it sounds—pastry dough that you press into the bottom of a pan—and yields a lovely, crunchy base for many sweet tarts. The chocolate truffle pastry is a decadent variation on the press pastry. The crostada dough is a rolled sweet pastry that works great for any single- or double-crusted tart or pie. For more Tips on working with pastry, see the Tarts chapter (page 78).

01 · Pastry dough is not to be feared or avoided. Just treat it with respect and patience while you are making it, and it will reward you with good results.

02 · Take the time to measure accurately. Always consistently follow either the metric or the Imperial measurements in a recipe (never mix them up).

03 · Use your hands and get to know how the doughs should feel.

04 · Always let your pastry rest well-wrapped in the refrigerator for at least 1 hour or preferably overnight before using.

05 · Make sure all of your ingredients are cold before you begin, especially butter and other wet ingredients. During the summer months, I even put my flour and sugar in the refrigerator for 1 hour before using.

06 · When lining your tart pan or pie plate, always allow for a little shrinkage. I recommend allowing a ¼-inch (0.5 cm) margin above the edge of the pan.

07 · Always preheat your oven.

08 · Almond paste not only adds an interesting flavor and texture to recipes but also moisture. (It also acts as a natural preservative.)

tip
....
See my YouTube video on
how to make press pastry.

press pastry

makes one 9-inch (23 cm) tart shell

1⅓ cups	all-purpose flour	325 mL
¼ cup	granulated sugar	60 mL
⅛ tsp	fine sea salt	0.5 mL
½ cup	cold unsalted butter, cut into 1-inch (2.5 cm) cubes	125 mL
1	large free-range egg yolk, beaten	4

1. In a medium bowl, combine flour, sugar, and salt. Using a pastry cutter, cut in butter until mixture is the consistency of coarse sand. (If using a food processor, pulse flour, sugar, and salt until well combined. Add butter and pulse until mixture is the consistency of coarse sand. Transfer to a medium bowl.)
2. Drizzle the beaten egg yolk over the flour mixture and, using your hands, roughly work into the dough until well combined. Transfer to an airtight container and refrigerate or freeze until ready to use. Will keep for up to 1 week in the refrigerator and for up to 1 month in the freezer.

cream cheese pastry

makes one 9-inch (23 cm) tart shell

tip

Make sure the butter and cream cheese are very cold before you begin. Ideally, cut them into cubes and then refrigerate or freeze for another 10 minutes before adding to the food processer.

⅓ cup	cold unsalted butter, cut into ½ inch (1 cm) cubes	75 mL
½ cup	cold cream cheese, cut into cubes	125 mL
1 cup	all-purpose flour	250 mL
½ tsp	fine sea salt	2.5 mL

In a food processor fitted with the metal blade, combine butter, cream cheese, flour, and salt, pulsing until dough just begins to form a ball. Using a spatula, scrape dough onto a clean work surface. Using your hands, gather dough into a ball, then flatten slightly. Dust dough lightly with additional flour, wrap tightly in plastic wrap, then refrigerate for at least 1 hour. (The dough can be made a day in advance and will keep for up to 1 day in the refrigerator or for up to 1 month in the freezer.)

chocolate truffle press pastry

makes one 9-inch (23 cm) tart shell

½ cup	all-purpose flour	125 mL
⅓ cup	granulated sugar	75 mL
⅓ cup	unsweetened cocoa powder	75 mL
¼ cup	frozen unsalted butter, cut into ½-inch (1.25 cm) cubes	60 mL
1	large free-range egg yolk	1

1. In a food processor fitted with the metal blade, pulse flour, sugar, and cocoa until blended. Add butter and pulse until mixture is the consistency of coarse sand. Using a spatula, scrape into a medium bowl.
2. In a small bowl, whisk yolk. Drizzle yolk over dry ingredients and, using a fork or your fingers, quickly mix into the mixture (it should be very loose and remain the consistency of sand). Transfer to an airtight container and refrigerate for up to 1 week or freeze for up to 1 month.

sweet tart dough

makes two 9-inch (23 cm) tart shells

2 cups	all-purpose flour	500 mL
¼ cup	granulated sugar	60 mL
½ tsp	fine sea salt	2.5 mL
1 cup	cold unsalted butter, cut into ½-inch (1 cm) cubes	250 mL
¼ cup	ice water	60 mL

1. In a food processor fitted with the metal blade, pulse flour, sugar, and salt until well combined. Add butter and pulse 12 to 14 times, until butter pieces are the size of small peas. With motor running, add water all at once and process for about 15 seconds, or until dough starts to come together.
2. Turn dough out onto a clean work surface and divide into 2 equal portions. Using your hands, form into rough balls and then pat into disks. Wrap in plastic wrap and refrigerate until chilled, at least 1 hour. Will keep for up to 2 days in the refrigerator and for up to 3 weeks in the freezer.

tip

The key to good pastry is not to handle it too much and to let it rest before rolling, which allows the gluten to relax and results in a lighter, more tender, crust.

almond paste

makes 2½ cups (625 mL)

2 cups	blanched slivered almonds	500 mL
½ cup	granulated sugar	125 mL
2	large free-range egg whites	2
¼ cup	unsalted butter, softened	60 mL
2 tsp	pure almond extract	10 mL

In a food processor fitted with the metal blade, pulse almonds and sugar until fine powder. Add egg whites, butter, and almond extract and pulse until mixture comes together into a ball. Turn out onto a piece of plastic wrap and, using your hands, form into a log. Wrap tightly and refrigerate until ready to use. Will keep for up to 1 week in the refrigerator or for up to 3 months in the freezer.

tip

Making almond paste is often a lot easier than trying to buy it. It can be hard to find and is often only available during the holiday season (when it is used to make marzipan to cover fruitcakes).

libby's peanut butter dog treats

makes about forty-two 3½-inch (9 cm) dog biscuits

Libby is my dog and I like to make her "dessert,"
too. She finds the peanut butter in these treats
completely irresistible. The nice thing about making
your own biscuits is that you can size them to suit
your pup, big or small. Just make a big batch—your
furry companion will be glad you did.

1 cup	old-fashioned rolled oats	250 mL
2 cups	whole-wheat flour	500 mL
2 tbsp	finely chopped fresh parsley	30 mL
½ cup	non-fat powdered milk	125 mL
1 tbsp	olive oil	15 mL
2	extra-large free-range eggs	2
1 cup	natural, salted chunky peanut butter	250 mL
½ cup	cold water	125 mL

1. Preheat oven to 325°F (160°C). Line 2 baking
   sheets with parchment paper.
2. In a large bowl, combine oats, flour, parsley,
   dried milk, and salt. Add olive oil, eggs, and
   peanut butter and stir to combine (the mixture
   will be crumbly). Add just enough water to
   bring the dough together.
3. Turn dough out onto a clean work surface and
   roll out to about ¼ inch (0.5 cm) thick. Using a
   cookie cutter, cut out biscuits.
4. Transfer biscuits to prepared baking sheet and
   bake in preheated oven for 30 to 45 minutes,
   until dark golden brown (they should be dry
   and crisp all the way through). Remove pan
   from the oven and set aside to cool.

tip

These treats will keep for up to 1 month (if they
last that long) in an airtight container (make
sure they are totally dry before storing).

acknowledgments

This book is the result of many years running a catering business and specialty food store. During that time I had the opportunity to work with an amazing number of very talented pastry chefs and to offer what I feel was a unique array of desserts and baked goods that friends and clients still pine after. I thank all of you.

In particular, I want to acknowledge Jill Duggan and Bobbi Jo Robertson, who helped me to prepare all of the recipes in this book for the photo shoot. Other pastry chefs who were on the Lesley Stowe Fine Foods team for years include Dawn Lowes, April Quercia, Karen Bruk, and Eleanor Tsang, and executive chefs Renee Reese and Liz Zmetana.

THANKS ALSO GO TO...

Maggie Aro, my right and often left arm for over 20 years, who helped me grow the business. Maggie has and always will be a huge influence on me in the kitchen and in running and growing Lesley Stowe Fine Foods.

Danielle Acken, who provided all of the gorgeous photography in this book and was my guiding light in making it happen, affording me the time to do it. Thank you for wearing so many different crowns along the way.

My Raincoast Crisps team, who through their belief in everything that we should do to be the best never compromise on service or the quality of the products.

Maybo Wu, who has worked with me for over 16 years. Everyone shows up for lunch when Maybo is in the kitchen!

My sister, Marianne, who was born in the fast lane and has always been able to sell anything she believed in. Whether desserts or Raincoast Crisps, she always inspires and motivates me to reach for the stars.

Suzanne Price, whose enthusiasm is infectious; Ali Samei, who brings order to our growing business; Susan McVee, Sheena Quish, Aysha Forgues, Craig Geitzen, Cindy Dunn, Chris Bray, and our whole production team, who make me proud and thrilled at what we have achieved.

Andrew Graham, who was a guiding light and voice of reason when things were going in ten directions. He's sharp with numbers and makes a mean gin and tonic.

Linda Yorke, one of my dearest friends and fellow foodie, in my life and kitchen since university days, who continuously inspires and feeds me. The photo shoot for this book couldn't have happened as smoothly without her accountant's brain. From spread sheets and purchasing, to prepping and cleaning, all along the journey she kept us in line. Her daughter, Adrienne, is falling close behind, even sharing her best-ever cheese scone recipe with me (sorry, you will have to wait for the next book for that one).

My book club, which is actually a food club in disguise. We don't just have dessert, but a full dinner every time we get together (the theme usually spun from any and all references to food in the book we have just read). Most club members are extremely accomplished cooks and/or have worked in the food profession: Linda Yorke, Kelly Lindahl, Pam Dennis, Ginny Love, Leigh Sauder, Anne Rowland, Nancy Hamilton, Corrine Jefferson, Alison Lambert, Jennifer O'Callaghan, Judy Bates, and Liz Jacobson. Thank you for always keeping the bar high.

Fellow members of Les Dames d'Escoffier—a group of hugely talented women who constantly strive to better the world through different channels, from teaching children how to cook to holding triages, from helping in community kitchens to writing and developing better products—have always played a role in influencing me. In particular I want to thank Becky Paris Turner, Pam Williams, Caren McSherry, Suzy Meister, Mary Mackay, Cate Simpson, Suzanne Ross, Margaret Chisolm, Nicky Major, Lee Murphy, Glenys Morgan, and Diane Clements.

Mary Butterfield, who introduced me to the world of Julia Child before I even dreamed I would have a career in food. I would pour over Mary's collection of books while babysitting her children, one of whom (Stephanie) ended up bringing her boundless energy to our kitchen.

So many friends and clients that I can't begin to name them all. As a start, thanks to Doris Daughney, whose summertime Sunday Bocci lunches with friends were remarkable for their themes (all white, Tuscan, Provençal, to name a few). Ed Daughney, Beth and Michael Noble, Carol and Richard Henriques, Diane and John Norton, Gail and John West, Barbara and David Gillanders, Nina and John Cassils, Wendy and George Rifel, Ginny and John Richards, Cathy and Peter Gudewill, Jackie and Bill Bevis, Janice and Hank Ketcham, and Leslie and Rob Mackay have been friends, students, and loyal clients.

The girls at Bacci's, who were so supportive, particularly Andrea Molnar, who loaned many of the gorgeous pieces used in the photography for this book from her fabulous store.

Sabine Wood, who loaned me her precious china and linens and throws such delicious dinner parties.

Leslie Young, my hair stylist, whose mother, Barbara, shared her white-chocolate apricot biscotti with me when I couldn't get enough of them.

Friends who have tested, ate, and supported me in my pursuit of not counting calories but counting flavor (thanks to the trainers at Innovative Fitness: Kevin, Todd, Cara, Ben, and Casey): Eric Savics, Wendy and Andy Hamilton, Jenny and Ricky Whittall, Linda and Gord Forbes, Nicky and Doug Seppela, Barb and Rob

Kemp, Jill and Hart Price, Deb and Hugh Notman, Sylvia and Peter Hart, Robert Lemon, Jill and David Lyall, Vivian Thom and Jim Green, Marian and Craig Tennant, Lisa and Mike Hudson, Elpie Marinakis, Annabel St. John, John and Susan Rose, Kathy and Denny Molnar, Jim and Doreen MacIvaney, Katie Zeidler, Peter Mackenzie, and Cindy Richmond.

The artists who influence me every day: Gordon Smith, Ian Wallace, Owen Kydd, Marian Penner Bancroft, Chris Dikeakos, Stan Douglas, Myfanwy MacLeod, Rodney Graham, Jeff Wall, and Ed Burtynsky.

The chefs who influence me every day: Vikram Vij, David Hawksworth, Rob Feenie, Pino Posteraro, John Bishop, Umberto Menghi, Tojo-san, Greg Hook, Thomas Hass, Susur Lee, Mark McEwan, Jamie Kennedy, David Chang, Thomas Keller, Suzanne Goin.

The retailers that believed in and supported us from the beginning: Whole Foods (Kathy Strange), Les Amis de Fromage (Alice and Alison), Gourmet Warehouse (Caren McSherry), Urban Fare and Overwaitea, Janice Beaton Fine Cheese, The Cookbook Co., Summerhill Market, All the Best Fine Foods (Susan and Jane), La Fromagerie Atwater (Gilles).

A special thanks to Peter and Chris Neal for their amazing team and their devotion to providing such incredible support and keeping it exciting every day.

George Deegan, who is my eyes and ears on the ground in Calgary. Thank you for all your support and wisdom.

The amazing team Sarah Scott, my publisher, assembled to produce this book: Tracy Bordian, my editor, you are a saint for putting up with my questions and stretched timelines and making the recipes flow consistently. Mauve Pagé, thank you for translating my vision, for the gorgeous layout, for sharing your experience and creativity.

My family, who have been my most ardent supporters since my first Apple Charlotte attempt at age 12: my mother; Marianne; Rob, Alexa, and Mackenzie Thomson; Craig and Sebastian Stowe; Nadia Ladisernia; Bruce Johnstone; Diane and Don Merson; and all my cousins. To the enormous Scott family: Janet, Sarah and David, Martha and Fred, Mary and Jim, Peter, and Jane; Tom and Laurie and their children; and the first great-granddaughter (many more soon to come) after whom I named the Charlotte Bars on page 59.

My favourite four-legged golden, Libby Noel, who greets all the guests and keeps the kitchen floor clean.

My husband, Geoffrey, who has put up with hours, days, weeks of me in the kitchen (does caramel sauce go with every dessert?) and at the computer with love, patience, and dinner reservations. The roi du bbq.

My learning and inspiration come from our children, Douglas and Gillian.

index